The Holy Seed

The Holy Seed:

OR, THE

LIFE

OF

Mr. Thomas Beard.

Wrote by Himself:

With some Account of his Death,
September 15. 1710.

Soon after he had ~~compleated~~ the
17th Year of his Age.

WITH HIS

Funeral Sermon.

By Jos. Porter.

With a Preface by the late Reverend Mr *Matth Henry*.

The THIRD EDITION, *with* Enlargements from his own Manuscript.

LONDON. Printed for NATH. CLIFF, at the Bible and three Crowns near Mercers Chappel in *Cheapside*, and D. JACKSON, at the Bible and three Crowns in the *Poultry*. 1715.

TO

Mr. *Richard Beard*,

BROTHER

TO THE

DECEASED.

SIR,

I Have at your Requeſt,
ventur'd abroad into
the World, the Minutes
of your Dear Brother's
Life, left under his own
A 2   Hand,

Hand, and his Funeral Sermon: Tho' I am senfible the whole Work is too plain for a *Curious*, and too ferious for a *Vain* Age.

It is not indeed all; yet all I can well collect; it being wrote in Characters, and for his own private Ufe, with fecret References.

I doubt not but it will be very grateful to you, tho' not in its Perfection: And I am fure if it be as affecting to others, as to my felf, it can't fail of being confiderably ufeful.

One

One thing I am willing to take this Opportunity to mind you of, That you are now the laſt *Remain* of a very Religious Race; on Father's ſide and Mother's ſide Religious; which 'tis eaſy to tiace thiough many Generations. May you live to propagate ſerious Piety yet fuither, and may it deſcend to the utmoſt Date of the Family. Foi, 'twould be very unhappy, if that Family ſhould ever iun Dregs, which hath been ſuch a Spiing of *pure and Chryſtalline Streams.*

A 3   That

The Dedication.

That the Divine Providence may direct you, and the Grace of God fix you, in that Poſt in which you may beſt anſwer the Character of the *Holy Seed,* called forth, and now left alone to ſerve the Lord Jeſus, is the ſinceie Wiſh of,

S I R,

Your moſt Affectionate

Servant,

Joſ. Porter.

T C

TO THE

READER.

Eing favour'd with the Perusal of these Papers in Manuscript, by means of my Acquaintance with that Family, of which this Pious Young Man was a promising Branch; I am willing to say with what Pleasure I read them, and to recommend them to those of the rising Generation among us, for whose real Service and Benefit they are design'd.

It

It was an observable Method which both our Blessed Lord, and his Apostles sometimes took; to Preach a Sermon first, and then work a Miracle, for the Confirmation of it: Or to work a Miracle first, and then preach a Sermon for the Improvement of it. Miracles are now ceas'd, but (blessed be God) Preaching is not, nor the Power of the Spirit, *Confirming the Word by Signs following of another Nature. You have here a very pathetical, serious Sermon; design'd to engage all young People, and particularly the Children of Godly Parents, to be betimes Religious: And you have here join'd with it, a bright and eminent example of early Piety, and that to a Miracle of Divine Grace, which the Sermon both gives the Improvement of, and receives Confirmation from.*

How

How powerful the Influence of ad Examples is, to corrupt and lebauch, we see daily: I am wiling to hope, that this, and other he like good Examples, may have a happy Influence upon some, by the Grace of God, to provoke them to a holy Emulation, and may erve both as the plainest Dire-ctions, and strongest Perswasives to all the Instances of serious God-iness; for it is not the Interest of any Party that this is intended to serve, but that of Pure Religion, *only unmix'd and* undefiled before God and the Father.

The Reflections which this Thinking, Praying Youth made upon his own Life, then, when he had but few Years to reflect upon; are here given you as they ought to be, in their own native Plain-ness and godly Simplicity; **and tho' consider'd in themselves, there**
may

*may be thought nothing extraordi-
nary in them, that they should de-
serve to be publish'd; yet look'd
upon, as coming from one of Six-
teen or Seventeen Years of Age,
they are really uncommon, and upon that Account one may hope,
will be the more taken Notice of
by those of that Age · and to a
good Christian, one truly* pious
*Thought is worth ten fine Thoughts.
And the Publishing of them may
help to make some little Amends,
for the mighty Loss we sustain'd
by the Death of one, that was so
likely to have been serviceable to
his Generation. Nay, they may
serve for a Copy to the ripest and
oldest Christians, and may shame
many that have doubled and tre-
bled his Years, and yet are not so
well acquainted as he was with
their own Spirits. The Books
which that Learned and Vertuous
Emperour,* Marcus Antoninus,
wrote τὰ ἑαυτὸν concerning himself,

elf, *and* to himself *are very va-*
uable Peices of Antiquity. And
we shou'd all find our Hearts bet-
er, if we did more frequently re-
ire into them; and our Lives bet-
er, if we did more frequently re-
flect upon them.

Perhaps, *if there were such a*
Collection of the most remarkable
instances of Devotion, in those
that were about the Age of this
young Man, both which have been
publish'd, and which might be ga-
ther'd up from credible Reports,
is there is of those in the earlier
Age, by Mr. White, *in his* Little
Book for Little Children, *and*
Mr. Janeway, *in his* Token for
Children; *it might be as useful*
in its Kind, as these have been
to the Age for which they were cal-
ulated. St. John *writes distinct-* 1 John 2.
y to Little Children, *and to* 12, 13.
Young Men.

That

To the Reader.

That God by his Grace would make the next Generation, wiser and better than this, and qualify many to be a Seed to serve Chrift, that from the Womb of the Morning he may have the Dew of their Youth, *and the Church the bleffed Fruits of that Dew, through a long Day, and that the* Firft ripe Fruits *which* our Souls defire, *may not be* nipt, *as here they were, in the Bloffom, is the Defire and Prayer of.*

A hearty Well-wifher to the Rifing Generation,

C H E S T E R,
March 1. 1710-11.

Matth. Henry.

A SHORT

ACCOUNT

OF THE

Memorable Passages

OF MY

LIFE,

THOMAS BEARD.

Give him thy Grace, **O** *God*

WHILST I declare the Passages of my Life, O Holy, Eternal, Gracius God, may thy Grace attend me, that I may be affected, O! deeply affected, with my own Cafe : With thy Mercies, O Lord ; and my Sins (Father) against Heaven,

B

ven, and before thee I humbly
thank thee for all thy Mercies, and
beg thy Pardon for all my Sins;
for thy dear Son's fake, fend me
thy Holy Spirit to work a thorough
Work of Grace in me; and to affift
me in this prefent great Work;
that this Book, this Paper, this
Leaf, may never come in as a Witnefs againft me at the laft. The
Lord help me, that tho' my former
Experiences have been of my
Weaknefs, yea Sinfulnefs; yet thofe
for the Time to come may be of
my Growth in Grace, and in the
Knowledge of my Lord and Saviour Jefus Chrift. And now, O
God the Father, God the Son, and
God the Holy Ghoft; I freely
give my Self, my Soul, my Body,
my All, unto thee, and for ever
refting upon thy Mercies in Jefus
Chrift, to whom, to thee, and the
Holy Spirit of Grace, be Praife,
everlafting Praife; for thine is the
Kingdom, the Power, and the
Glory, for ever and ever, Amen,
and Amen.

CHAP.

CHAP I.

Of my Birth-Privileges.

THE firſt and earlieſt Reflections I can make, are upon
the many and great Privileges of
my Birth. I can trace the Foot-
ſteps of the Grace of God from the
very Womb. O would to God I
had a Tongue to ſpeak forth his
Praiſe : And a Heart ſuitably affected with that Love, that Happineſs, that attended me from my
very Birth Attend O my Soul !

1. I was born in a profeſſing,
reform'd, religious Nation What
a Mercy ! Had I been born a Turk,
a Jew, a Papiſt, a Heathen, I
might have liv'd and died ſuch ;
but bleſſed be God, I was born in
a Proteſtant Goſpel-Land, under
the Means of Grace

2 I was not indeed born in a
Noble Family. Had it been ſo, I
might have devoted my ſelf to the
Pleaſures and vain Faſhions of the
World, which I find my own In-
B 2   clinations

clinations lead me to, and thus aspiring after Greatness here, I might have complimented my Soul into everlasting Misery.

The World is a bewitching Thing : It is hazardous moving in the highest Spheres My Lot fell where I am less expos'd, and better 'secur'd. I was, I bless my God, born of Parents, who had an agreeable Competency of the good Things of this World, and knew how to dispose of them for the Noblest Purposes A sanctified Sufficiency is good Provision, yea the best Portion.

3. Yea, that which is more valuable. I was born of religious Parents, truly religious : Thanks, O Thanks be to God It is a greater Mercy to be born of good Parents' than of Princes I was not born of Erroneous Parents, who have Zeal without Knowledge, and the Shew of Religion, without the Power and Purity of it ; who might have leaven'd my early Years with false Notions; and so have lead me out of the Way of God, into the Bypaths of Sin ; for Errors in Judgment,

nent, naturally produce Errors
n Practice, and seldom one Error
ous alone, for its *Name is Legion*,
cause they *are many* But I was
born of Parents who were Ortho-
dox and Sound in the Faith, who
had a good Report of all Men, and
of the Truth it self: Whose Joy it
would have been, to have seen
their Children walking in the
Truth O that I may be a Child
of Light, and not of Darkness I
was born of Parents eminent for
practical Godliness, holy, humble,
obedient, attending constantly on
all the Ordinances of God, confor-
mable in their Lives to all his holy
Laws, who had all the Marks of
grown Christians, in Life and in
Death, who are now, I doubt not,
praising God in the eternal World,
O that I may be a faithful Follower
of them, as they were of Christ:
That I may with them for ever and
ever adore that distinguishing
Love, that saved them, and I
hope will save me too O Lord
so let it be. I was born of Praying Parents, eminent in their Duty; many a Petition did they put

B 3 up

up to Heaven for me, and my poor
Brother. How oft, how earneftly
did they beg for Mercy for theirs,
that they might meet them with
Comfort in the Great Day of the
Lord, when Theirs had faithfully
ferved God, and Their Generation.

"O Lord take down the Files,
" view over their Prayers, and re-
" member the Children of thy Ser-
" vants now in Glory." The Prayers of Parents for their Children,
are better than the Eftates of Parents   May I never crofs nor cancel one Petition. I was born of
charitable Parents, of whofe Cha-
rity both the Church and Strangers
were Witneffes, who being dead,
yet fpeak. They were free with
their Money to fupply the Neceffi-
ties, and highly charitable with
good Books to the Souls of Sinners,
that they might encourage true Religion. A very confiderable Portion of every Year's Increafe was
fet apart for charitable Ufes, and
God was pleafed to profper them in
all their wordly Concerns. Cha-
rity never goes unrewarded in this
Life.

ife. May I learn of them as a
ear Child

I was born of moſt indulgent,
nder, careful Parents, who not
ut of Cuſtom, but ſincerely and
eartily gave me up with them-
lves to God, in Covenant, in
eir private Devotion, and in the
ublick Ordinances : Both in Bap-
ſm, and frequently at the Table
f the Lord. How can I go back ?
The Vows of God are upon me. I
m thine, O Lord, by the moſt
arly Dedication, and thine may I
e for ever and ever.

It pleas'd God to remove my
ear Parents, when I was very
oung, ſo that I never remember
hem. I have only heard who they
ere, and how they liv'd : I wait
o know more in the other World.
was about three Years old when
y God took from me my deareſt
arents, almoſt at the ſame time;
o that I was Fatherleſs and Mo-
herleſs in my very Infancy, but
not Friendleſs ; for my God took
me up, as if he deſign'd to take the
ſole Care of me himſelf; and a very peculiar Regard he had to me.

B 4   " Lord

" Lord fill up the Relations
" Death hath diffolv'd, be a Fa-
" ther to the Fatherlefs, and ten-
" der, with the Love of a Mother,
" the Motherlefs " A Heavenly
Father is the beft Father, an everlafting Father. A precious Redeemer, is the beft Relation Lord
grant me my Defires, and fulfil thy
Promifes to thy Servant, that is devoted to thee Amen.

Sure, all Advantages confider'd,
no one Individual in the World
hath had greater and better Birth-
Privileges than I: O that I may
never profanely fell my Birth-
Right, but anfwer it with the
higheft Improvements.

My dear Parents took great Care
for my holy Education, which the
Lord profper At their Death,
they committed me to the Care
and Infpection of thofe, who they
knew would not only be concern'd
for the Welfare of my Body, but
principally of my precious Soul.
And thus in my Minority, was I
left in kind and faithful Hands, and
efpecially in the kindeft Hands of
my deareft Lord : O how ought I
to

to love and refpect the Memory of my dear Parents : Holy Parents deferve the beft Love, and Obedience whilft Living, and the moft Honourable Remembrance when dead. May I never do any thing unworthy of them. But moft of all I owe my felf to my deareft Redeemr O my Soul, thefe Bleffings Chrift procur'd for me with his own Blood Admire him and Love him, and do him all the Service thou canft in the World. O Lord, grant I may meet my Holy Parents, and Gracious and Glorify'd Friends, with Comfort in the other World, at the great Day, when I believe I fhall fee them again May I be their Crown of Joy in that Day. Bleffed Parents and Childreu, and Families, that meet together at laft in Chrift, and with Chrift for ever

CHAP.

C H A P. II.

Of my Education.

THUS at the Defire of my now glorified Parents, and by the Providence of my Heavenly Father, my Lot was caft here at *Aulcefter* in *Warwickfhire,* where I am to praife God, in the midft of a Thoufand Enjoyments

This is a Place moft free from the common Temptations of the World I have here no ill Company to infect me, no ill Examples to corrupt me, no Swearers, no Curfers, no Drunkards, no Sabbath-breakers, no prophane Scoffers; None but what Pray, and are obliged to keep conftant to their private Duty as well as their publick Attendances Here are indeed the common Vanities of Youth, but few, but who feem to favour the beft things; and none of my Affociates, but who I hope are truly ferious The Frowardnefs of fome, is for my Tryal and Exercife : and the Serioufnefs of others, for my Encouragement

ragement. O Bleſſed be God, that my Lot ſhould be caſt here. A good Family is a good City of Refuge.

I fell into the Hands of a moſt tender, loving, ſkilful, compaſſionate Maſter; a Father rather than a Maſter, whoſe Endeavour hath been to train me up in Learning, and in the Fear of the Lord together One that knew patiently to bear with my puerile Infirmities: But yet faithfully corrected me for greater Miſcarriages: But never in a Paſſion, always with Meekneſs and Tenderneſs: With Love convincing me of my Error, and affecting me with a Senſe of my Fault. Gentle Rebukes are ſovereign Medicines, and kind Correctors choice Friends. We all not only fear, but love our Maſter. Meer Fear is ſlaviſh, but Love and Fear are truly Generous. Good Maſters are publick Bleſſings Here I have ſat under the powerful Diſpenſations of all the Ordinances of God, for above fourteen Years together, I have heard the joyful Sound; I have heard ſuch Sermons, and ſuch Subjects, that have been

enough

enough to awaken the moſt ſtupid, and affect the moſt dull; which I am ſure have had many Seals How ſweet hath the Word been to my Taſte, I earneſtly remember it ſtill. May I prove one of the Seals of this Miniſtry. Good Miniſters are ſome of the greateſt Mercies to the World O my Soul, bleſs God for ſuch Soul Friends

Here I have had the Privilege of Family-Worſhip Thrice a Day have I heard the Word read; and Prayers offer'd Once a Week have I heard one or other Queſtion in Religion examin'd and ſtated. Once a Week have I been catechiſed and inſtructed Once a Week have I had an Opportunity of more publick Prayer Twice a Week, ſince I have had any Capacity, I and my Companions have privately engag'd in Prayer together, and here I have met with God Twice every Sabbath have I heard Practick Preaching, and in the Evening Repetition. Theſe, unleſs any thing extraordinary hath interrupted, have been my conſtant Privileges for many Years What an Account have I

to

to give, O my Soul! How shall I answer it to God, Lord help me, that my Improvements may be according to my Enjoyments. Here, O my Soul, stand and admire at the Love of God in Christ, and his Free Grace to me; that whilst Thousands perish for want of Knowledge, I should be train'd up in the School of Christ Few in the World have had half my Privileges Should I perish under such Enjoyments, how low should I sink in Misery God forbid.

I came here very Young, and so had good Principles instill'd into me, before the Vanities of the World had insinuated themselves. I had a Closet to retire into, for private Devotion, and Heart Examination; I have had some of the choicest Books to Read, almost on every Subject I have had time enough allow'd me for Soul-concerns; O that I had improv'd it as I ought I have not wanted Encouragement, Counsels, Exhortations to what is Good, nor Restraints from what is Evil. Yea, here I have had the gracious Assistances

of

of the Spirit of God. Thefe and
a Thoufand more have been my
choice Privileges. Had I impro-
ved them as I ought, I might have
been one of the firft, one of the moft
eminent of Chriftians of my Age
and Standing. Lord! How fhall I
anfwer it? Good Education is like
a good Foundation for the beft Su-
perftructure. Millions have been
ruined by bad Education. How
mercifully hath the Grace of God
confulted my Happinefs. Happy
indeed, if thofe of us, that have
been educated together, anfwer
our Education: O that there may
not be a prophane *Efau* among all
the Flock

But this is not all the Happinefs
I have met with here. The Providence of God plac'd me in the
Arms and Bofom of a tender Mi-
ftrefs, who took as much Care of
me, as mine own Mother would
have done. Thus when one Mother was dead, God provided me
another, that I was but a little
while Motherlefs Had my own
Parents liv'd, perhaps I had never
been planted in this Family, my
own

own good Mother, as I have heard, being exceedingly indulgent, which I might foolishly have abused to my own Prejudice. O the Myſteries of Divine Goodneſs, even in the darkeſt Providences God ſpeaketh out of the Clouds; his very Frowns oft prove great Bleſſings And becauſe my Miſtreſs exceſſively indulged me, my God foreſeeing I might have miſimprov'd ſuch Kindneſs, was pleas'd to remove her too Thus I loſt two Mothers, but my God ſtill cared for me May I meet them both at laſt at the Right Hand of Chriſt Exceſſive Indulgence oft proves prejudicial to poor Minors. Fond Friends are not always the beſt Friends: But I was not left Friendleſs What turns did the Wheels of Providence take for my Advantage, I can't but admire, and ſay, O Wheel! O Bleſſed be God for his correcting Mercies Lord help me ſeriouſly to conſider the Privileges that I have had: Aſſiſt me, O my God *Amen.*

CHAP.

CHAP. III.

Of the Vanity of my Youth.

WHO in the World hath more to anfwer for than I? but what Account fhall I give? I have reafon to lament, and fay, *Childhood and Youth are Vanity* The Lord forgive me From the Age of Three, to Twelve Years old, there was little or nothing but Vanity. I was pleas'd with every puerile Impertinence and Trifle : But Religious Exercifes were without Guft and Savour I was devoted to my Sports and Paftimes, extravagantly fond of Gaming . This was my very Element I moved in, whilft the precious Soul was fhamefully neglected, and expofed. Thus I ventur'd the Lofs of all, to gratify my own Humours and flefhly Inclinations Flefh Pleafers are bold Adventures. How much precious Time did I wafte in thefe filly Frolicks. I was a true Drudge to fenfual

al Pleafures Night and Day con-
riving, forecafting, flaving at
hem.

Was Time no more precious?
Had I taken that Pains in ferving
my God, as in ferving the Flefh,
hat Joy and Comfort might I have
ow had! But O how afflictive are
he Thoughts of thefe things? Sin
nd Satan are ill Mafters I was
oon tired with that which is Good,
ut unwearied at my Sports I
hought I might have been excufed,
ecaufe Young, but Confcience
ill not excufe. O that the God
f Confcience would forgive me.

The blackeft Crime I have to
harge my felf with, is the hor-
id Sin of Lying Which tho'
ut rarely committed, and to ex-
ufe my felf too; yet how do the
houghts of it fting me! What a
ile Wretch was I? What a young
inner? Lies do not extenuate,
ut double the Fault

I was often admonifhed, and ferioufly called upon; but I was deaf
to Counfel: And tho' I fometimes
fmarted for it, yet my Inclinations
were fo ftrong, and violent, that I
pufht

pufht on in gratifying the Flefh.
What a finful Nature have I? How
is Folly bound up in my Heart?
The more Warnings, the greater
the Sin

I did not indeed live without
Duty. I was not fuffered, or elfe
my own corrupt Nature would
gladly have difpens'd with it. I
had Books more for a Shew, than
Service, I was covetous of Books,
but feldom read in them Books
without Grace to ufe them, are a
poor Library I fometimes retired
into my Clofet, but what did I
there? Little better I fear than wafte
part of my Time in Vanity The
moft I can fay is, I was there; O
that I could fay, I had been with
God there

Indeed whilft I was thus bufie
at Vanity, and drudging for Trifles,
my Confcience often, or always
checkt me, I was afhamed of my
felf Sin always carries Guilt and
Shame with it, whilft Duty afford-
eth true Peace and Satisfaction. I
had often too, fome gracious Motions, and Divine Influences; but
the childifh Humour, and brutifh
Flefh

efh bore all down. I oppofed
onfcience, I quenched the Spi-
t, I flighted Admonitions, to ful-
the Defires of the Flefh, which
ow cofts me dear. Alas! alas!
welve Years of my fhort Life
ve been wafted and loft. The
ord forgive me

CHAP. IV.

my firft Acquaintance with God.

BUT God was more merciful
to me, than I was to my felf.
was Vain and Sinful, and deftroy-
ng my felf; but God's Grace ap-
ear'd to me. God's Grace is a
etter Preferver than our own Re-
lutions 'Tis fomewhat to be born
ithin the Virge of the Covenant.
Vhen I was between Twelve and
Thirteen Years old, the Grace of
God laid hold on me: It found me
rifling, but it quickly made me fé-
ious: It found me Worldly, but
t quickly made me Heavenly; I
emember the time.. I fhall never
forget

forget the Day The Day of our
Converſion ought never to be for-
got It was on a Saturday, I think,
An Dom 1704 The Day of my
Eſpouſals, and of the Gladneſs of
my Heart.

By the Direction of my dear
Maſter, ſome of greater Maturity
than I retired to pray together, to
help forwards one another's Salvation; Poor I happily was in their
way, but buſy at my Sports One
of them, my dear Friend, the happy Inſtrument, asked me to go with
them : And I being proud of Eſteem,
was ambitious to aſſociate with
them, not knowing as far as I can
recollect, what their Deſign was.
Had I known it had been for Prayer, I fear I ſhould have choſe my
Diverſions But God had a great
Work to do in me, and for me :
how free, how rich, how wonder-
ful is the Grace of God ! Whilſt
they were engaged in Duty, I did
little elſe but laugh behind the
Curtain. Thus I came away, not
the better, but the worſe, had not
the Grace of God over-ruled (O
my Soul behold and admire the
good

ood Hand of my God upon me)
oon after, I overheard two or
hree cenfuring me, for my inde-
ent Atheiftick Carriage, and my
heart inftantly fmote me   O fee
ow the Stratagems of Satan fome-
imes through Grace become the
Means of Salvation ! He defigned
 for Evil, but the Grace of God
ver-ruled it to my everlafting Wel-
re · Thus the good Work began,
d my Repentings were kindled
gether   My Heart burned with-
 me   One of my Companions
as fo faithful to me, as to reprove
e ferioufly, and fpeak to me af-
ctionately about another World ;
d the Spirit of God fet in with
e kind Admonitions : Every Ex-
effion came with Power, forth-
th I refolved to fet on the great
ork of Salvation   O fee, my
ul, what God can do ? *Out of the*
outh of Babes and Sucklings he or-
neth Strength, to ftill the Enemy,
d the Aveng.
That which help'd on the good
ork, was the good Company I
d. It pleafed God at this very
e to work upon the Confciences

ces of almoſt all our Claſs : Wh
had all a very great Concern upo
us, for our own, and one anothe
Souls, our precious and immort
Souls. We had each others Exam
ples and Prayers to help on one
nother to Heaven and Glory : (
how ſweet was it to talk with m
Companions of an everlaſtin
State ! How much was I affecte
with their Diſcourſes. Thus
walked together as Brethren, ed
fying one another, and drawir
one another nearer and neaier
God in a Way of Duty Goo
Examples are good Guides
Heaven

What further advanc'd the goo
Work, was a happy Dream I h
one Night as I lay on my Bed.
dreamt that I ſaw the Tribunal
God erected, and all brought to
Bar , and all my Companions
cepted, and bleſſed, and carr
up to the Enjoyment of God
Heaven : But I, poor miſerą
Wretch, was left behind T
dreadful Thought ſtruck me w
Terror and Horror · It was as
He'l begun I ſoon awoke, b

ny Dread hung upon me; I con-
inued amazed, yet blessing God I
was out of Hell, resolving, with
reat Diligence, to set upon the
Work of my eternal Salvation. O
he Love of God, in guiding my
Thoughts in the Night Season!
Dreams themselves, thro' the Grace
f God, may be Helps to Heaven.
When the Morning came, I arose,
rangely surpriz'd with my present
ate, I quickly fell to my Prayers,
d pour'd out my Soul to God, the
ord hear every Petition. Amen.
My Affection and Zeal for Re-
gion was soon taken notice of by
y dearest Master, who took oc-
sion to talk sweetly and heavenly
me, and to encourage me to go
with such Expressions as these:
hat, my dear Child, dost in good
rnest begin to look after God?
ejoice in thee, and over thee:
hat! Looking Heaven-wards. O
on, let nothing discourage, nor
nder thee · This, this is the way
thy glorified Parents. What
ll I be so happy as to present thee
last to them, my Joy, and their
y, my Crown, and their Crown;

and

and the Joy of God, and Chrift fo
ever Such Expreffions foon melt
ed down my Heart, drew Tear
from me I thank'd him, and ask'
him for fome good fuitable Book
he foon directed me, and fupplie
me, and with many Encourage
ments and Affurances of Accep
tance with God, prefs'd me to g
on I remember it ftill O wha
Bleffings are good Advifers, an
tender Confciences.

I now began, with great Seri
oufnefs, to think of the beft Things
The Spirit of God gracioufly gui
ded my Thoughts. It came pow
erfully into my Mind, what
Wonder of Mercy I was : Tha
whilft thoufands perifh'd in the
S.ns, the free Grace of God fhoul
lay hold on me · That I fhould b
fpar'd, and they cut down, tha
had not finned againft fuch Light
fuch Mercies, and Privileges, an
Warnings, as I O what a Mer
cy, that fuch a Wretch as I fhoul
be owned, who had fo fhamefull
flighted the Grace of God !
what a Mercy, that as I adde
one Slight to another, God did no
ad

dd one Judgment to another!
That my Dream did not prove
Reality, that I should be on this
ide Misery, who might have been
ondemned for ever Still I am
pared Lord help me, that I
may improve the Day of thy Pa-
ience

I soon observ'd the malicious De-
igns of Satan against me He hath
peculiar Spite against the Chil-
ren of good Parents, and of pious
ducation If such a one as I pe-
ish, it will be with a Witness· My
all will be greater than that of
oft in the World, as my Privile-
es have been greater The Fall
f the Posterity of the Righteous
moft scandalous and pernicious
themselves and others I have
e more need to watch, and pray,
d fight valiantly the Lord's Bat-
es, O help me *Amen*

This brought it warm on my
houghts, that the Providence of
od had plac'd me under happy
ircumstances, and at the very
ates of Salvation, descending
om gracious Parents. The God
f my dear Parents is willing to be

C   my

my God. He that was merciful to [...]
them, will be merciful to me, be[...]
ing one with them. I am one tha[...]
hath the faireſt Opportunity fo[...]
Heaven, I bleſs God, my Father[...]
God O forſake not the Son of th[...]
Handmaid God hath bleſſed m[...]
for their ſakes, even to Admiration[...]

The Deſigns of the Grace o[...]
God, muſt be my eternal Welfare[...]
for *he delighteth not in the Death of*[...]
Sinner, much leſs in the Death of on[...]
that is a Branch of a Religious Fa[...]
mily The preſent Bleſſings too [...]
beſtows upon Me, are great Aſſu[...]
rances of eternal Bleſſings H[...]
that is ſo kind now, will be eter[...]
nally kind, if I am not wanting t[...]
my own Soul If ever I periſh[...]
my Damnation will lie at my ow[...]
Door. There is Hope for me, an[...]
the beſt Encouragements O tha[...]
I may never reſt in the Creature[...]
but reſt upon the Creator

I have indeed been a very pro[...]
voking Wretch; there is no roo[...]
for delay; 'tis high time for me t[...]
reform, and ſet upon the grea[...]
Work, who have loitered and lin[...]
ned away ſo many Years. Th[...]
Spiri[...]

Spirit will not always strive with
me O now my Soul set in with
its Motions· God will not always
bear with me, no v then is the Time
to engage in the Service of my
God O now let me begin, and
close in with God, and accept him
for my God   *And* 1

Should I stifle all these Motions,
what would be the Issue ? Whom
Mercies win not, Judgments soon
overtake. Judgments hang over
their Heads, who despise the Grace
of God And it may be, those
judgments may not so much as
alarm me, if I not harden my
own Heart, but only serve to har-
en me for eternal Judgments

Wherefore I resolve instantly to
begin, whilst it pleaseth God to
deal with my Conscience Bles-
ed be the Lord, that hath met with
me in the Beginning of my Days,
whilst others are justly left to sin
on to Old Age, how free is the
Grace of God? Even so Father,
so it seemeth good in thy sight

Thus I set seriously to the main
Work, three times every Day I retired for private Devotion, and four

times every Lord's Day: When I
poured out my Soul to God in Prayer, besides Family and publick Attendances When Holiness is real,
it will shew it self in good Works

And whilst I thus walk'd with
God, I had not the least Sickness
I felt not the least Pain· I met not
with the least Trouble, as I know
of, though in a troublesome World,
unless this that I was a Sinner
The Lord pardon me

And O what sweet Communion
had I with God? What Delight
in Ordinances? How sweet to
think of another World, and of the
Love of Christ to my Soul? How
pleasant to talk of Everlasting Happiness? I had a Heaven upon
Earth, and thus it continued for a
long time And tho' the Festivals
come on, when our common Business was dismist; and I was called
abroad to visit my Friends, my
Heart in every Place was taken up
about another World: No Diversions jusled out Duty; I sought for
Retirements for Prayer, and Communion with God, and God heard
me. I returned to my old Post
with

with the fame Zeal and Life; and my growth in Knowledge, and in the Grace of God, was very vifible. Thus all things went well with me, whilft I kept clofe to God and Duty

---

CHAP. V.

Of my Decays and Apoftacy.

YET notwithftanding all my Privileges, Enjoyments, Hopes, Promifes, Attendances, Experiences, Encouragements, notwithftanding all thefe I fell: I fell foully and fhamefully. Oh I fell from God and my Duty Oh perfidious, vile, finful Wretch! I fell from that God, from whom I had received innumerable Favours, and Mercies. Oh the Deceitfulnefs of Sin! The Cunning of the Enemy! The Corruption of my own Heart

I durft not omit Duty, but I fell under a wretched Indifferency: I more rarely attended upon it, I

C 3 quickly

quickly became dull and ftupid:
Religious Exercifes loft their Sweet-
nefs: The Word of the Lord became the Burden of the Lord The
Spirit with-held its Influcnces, my
God withdrew from me   I was as
one deferted   I went backward
many degrees

And thus the Enemy deceiv'd
me, and prevail'd againft me, and
drew me into many Snares and
Sins. I return'd to my old Vanities, and wafted many precious
Hours in unbecoming Diverfions,
which I thought harmlefs, but the
Reflections prove bitter. O how
much Time did they devour, and
fomewhat of Treafure too, which
might have been better imploy'd.
This lead me into one more grofs
Miftake, to the wounding of my
Confcience, which I cannot but
continually lament. My Mind
was ftrangely fet upon my Pleafures, which I attended more con-
ftantly than my Duty   Thefe ftole
away my Affections from my God,
and my Duty. O Lord forgive me.
Amen.

The

The Caufes of my Apoftacy, fo far as I can recollect, were thefe two. It is good to fearch into the grounds of Apoftacy, that we may for the future avoid the Occafions of Sin, and no more fall from God.

The firft Stumbling-block was, the ill Example of fome of my dear Companions, who tho' hopeful and ferious whilft here, foon declin'd when abroad in the World. Which caft a Damp, not only upon my Spirits, but upon theirs who were left behind. Thofe that encouraged me to Serioufnefs, were the firft that difcourag'd me. It is one thing to be under the Influence of Religious Government, and another thing to be left to the wide World. Ill Examples, even at a diftance, are vaftly prejudicial. The Defection of hopeful Beginners is of the worft confequence to the Souls of others.

Many hopeful Buds have been nipt. Thus we who were Fellow-helpers of one another's Faith, became Deftroyers of the fame. May I ever take care of ill Company.

C 4   How

How eafily did they prevail againſt me, who by the Cunning of Satan fell away by degrees?

Another Occaſion of my Fall was, the Omiſſion of one known Duty, that I wilfully abſented from, and God juſtly withdrew I fee if I give way to one Sin, Satan will quickly draw me to another: And thus the who'e Link may run on, even to my eternal Condemnation, without the preventing *Grace* of God " O Lord, O Merciful " God, pardon and forgive, for e- " ever and ever *Amen*

My Soul, take care, and attend upon all the Ordinances of God, leaſt one Omiſſion ſhould run on to thy Eternal Damnation.

CHAP VI.

Of my Recovery.

BUT God who choſe me from my Mother's Womb, had Mercy upon me, and why on me, when others of my Companions

are

are hardened? Happy if this Relation prove to their Conviction.
" O Lord, let not Convictions die.
" O God, my God, let not Convi-
' ctions die *Amen.*

Praises to Restraining Grace.

What shall I now do, that I may no more prevaricate and turn aside? I will charge my Soul most earnestly, and bind my self for ever to the Lord, in a most solemn Covenant, and cast my self upon the Grace of God in Christ for ever

And now my Soul, that God's frequent Calls, and my Refusals and Apostacies, may not provoke the Spirit to withdraw, and leave me to the Commissions of my old Sins; and thus I become a greater Sinner, and hardned for ever, and be at last condemned at God's Bar. O my Soul, I charge thee to consider

How shall I be ever able in an unconverted Estate, to meet my glorified Father and Mother, with any Comfort in the Great Day of the Lord? And can I be content to be eternally parted from them? God forbid.

C 5 How

How can I bear the Wrath of God for ever?

What for ever be excluded Heaven and Happiness, and be shut up in the Flames of Hell to all Eternity! God forbid

All my Acquaintance, and Religious Companions, will come in as Witnesses against me, if I prove unsincere Oh dreadful! Oh dreadful! And my Master, and my God too, will implead me, before all the World And how shall I answer their Charges? I shall have all the Sorrows in the World upon me

But if I faithfully serve my God, my Parents, my Master, my Companions, and all will witness for me: My Conscience, my God will be for me. All will help me, if I am faithful; and all will be against me, if I am otherwise.

God hath promised that he will own me, if I return to him "O "my God, turn me Now, O Lord, "I come, accept me, O Lord Jesus."

Then shall I taste of the Sweetness of Religion. I shall have Peace of Conscience, Joy in the Holy Ghost,

Ghoft, Increafe of Grace, and Per-
feverance therein unto the end.
I fhall be bleffed in all my Studies
and Labours, and in all I have
God will hear my Petitions at all
times

I fhall be fat and flourifhing in
the Houfe of my God.

I fhall be profperous in all I have,
in all I do

I fhall have no Troubles to af-
flict me, but what will turn to my
Advantage I fhall be deliver'd
from an uncomfortable Death here,
and a miferable Death for ever
Lord, help, let thefe things invite
and draw me to thy felf *Amen*

I am thine, Lord, I am thine.

In the Prefence of the Great
God, I declare this **Day,**

That Four times every **Day, I**
will make my Application to him
for all Things

That whenever I am tempted, I
will run to him for Succour.

That I will not fuffer my felf to
be enthralled by any **Lufts in the**
Service of the Devil

That all I do fhall be referr'd to
the Glory of God.

That

That I will never profane his Holy Sabbaths

That I will be ferious in Reading, in Praying, in Hearing, in every Duty

I will never dare to tell a wilful Lye, *&c*

O Great God, enable me by thy Grace to obferve all thefe Things. Be pleafed to pardon all my Sins, and help me by thy Grace, who am refolved to endeavour to perform all that thou enjoineft me to do To which I put my Hand and Seal this Day.

T. B

My Beloved is mine, and I am his Let this be the Motto.

And the better to confirm my Soul, I will fubfcribe Mr *Allen's* Covenant, and that Covenant of Grace and Life, which my dear Mafter hath pen'd down for us, which is as followeth.

The

The Gospel Covenant.

I call Heaven and Earth to witness this Day,

That I renounce with Abhorrence all Idol-lovers whatsoever, and avouch the Great God of Heaven and Earth to be my Sovereign Lord and Happiness: To whom, and to whose Service, I devote my self for ever. For Sanctification, for Justification, for Consolation, for Preservation, and for Salvation.

First, I take God the Father to be my Sovereign Lord and Father, whose Interest I will espouse as mine own, and whose Will I will carefully attend, casting my self upon his rich Grace alone, through Jesus Christ my Lord

2 I take God the Son to be my Saviour, Lord, and Mediator, my Prophet, Priest and King; to whose Government I entirely yield my self, building all my Hopes of Happiness upon his meritorious Obedience, through the saving Operations of the blessed Spirit.

3. I

3 I take God the Holy Ghost to be my Sanctifier, Guide and Comforter: To whose Conduct I submit my self, depending upon his sacred Influences, according to the Word of God

4. I take the Word of God to be the Rule of my Faith, both of my Doctrines and Practice. I believe it to be a perfect Rule ; and resolve to conform my self to it as it is receiv'd in the Church of God

5 I take the Church of God to be my Habitation, resolving to associate with God's faithful Servants, in all the Institutions of his Grace, and to advance all I can the true Evangelical Protestant Religion in my Place and Generation.

6. I give my self to God the Father, Son and Spirit My Soul and Body, my Name and Estate, and all that is mine, to be at his Disposal and Service: Whose I am, and whose I desire all that is mine should be.

Thus I take the Great God to be my God, my Covenant-God, and the God of mine, in Covenant for evermore, according to the Riches
of

of his Grace in Jesus Chrift.

And all this I do, as in the Prefence of God, Angels, and Men, without Force, or Fraud, Referve, or Revocation

Amen and Amen So help me, O my God

To which, by thy Grace, I put my Hand and Seal.

T B. ●

My Beloved is mine, and I am his.

Lord God help me in renewing this Covenant; put my Heart into a Covenant Frame ; that I may ftand to it as long as I live. Amen and Amen

T B. ●

November 29. 1708. Before Men and Angels, I proteft to abide by what I have here wrote. Lord help me, that I may not go back; but ferioufly anfwer my Engagements. I take thee again to be my God.

T. B.

Lord

Lord enable me to keep my Covenant with all my Heart, all the
Days of my Life, that I may never
turn aside to serve the Enemy more,
which I resolve thro' Grace

T B

Lord help me by thy Spirit to
perform what thou requireſt, and
I have again and again covenanted
to do, *Amen*

There's need of renewing our
Covenants, if we will abide with
God.   But renewed Bonds without
Grace will never hold the deceitful
Heart   This, therefore being the
Seventeenth Year of my Age, *Au-
guſt* 20. 1709. and the Turning
Day of my Life, I deſire ſolemnly
to renew my Covenant.   The
Lord keep me, O keep me cloſe to
thy ſelf   *Amen.*

T B. ●

Seal, O ſweet Jeſus, Seal all to
my Soul, with the Blood of the e-
verlaſting Covenant, that I may
be thine, and for ever thine. Thine
I am, O Lord; help, O Good
God :

God : Help, O my Redeemer : Help
O my God · Help, O Jefus · Help,
O bleffed Spirit   Help, O God
the Father, Son and Holy Ghoft.
Seal, O God : Seal, O Lord Jefus :
Seal, O bleffed Spirit   O God the
Father, Son and Holy Ghoft, ac-
cept me, I befeech thee, my Fa-
ther, my Saviour, my Sanctifier ,
for thy Name's fake, for Jefus's fake,
for the Love of the Spirit   *Amen.*
Amen, Amen

And becaufe 'tis now fit I fhould
choofe fome Courfe of Life, in
which I may ferve my God, and
his Church, and my Generation,
upon mature Deliberation and
Thought, with the Counfel of my
deareft Friends, and agreeable, as
I am told, to the Defigns of my
now glorified Parents ; I folemnly
make Choice of the Work of the
Miniftry, to be the Work of my
Life, believing I have a Call from
God   And accordingly this Day
engage my felf to God, in his peculiar Service.

The

The Ministerial Covenant.

I do now in the Prefence of the Great God, Angels and Men, devote my felf, thro' the Affiftance of his Grace, to the Service of the Great God, refol ing to renounce the World, the Flefh, and the Devil ; and to love, honour and obey, to fubmit to, and truft in my God for ever, The Father, Son, and Holy Ghoft. And that I may in the clofeft and more particular Manner be feparated from the World, and be ferviceable to my God, and to my own and other's Souls, I am ambitious of his Grace, thro' whicn I may choofe the great Work of the Miniftry, to be the ftated Bufinefs of my Life: And refolve by his Grace, to be diligent and faithful in his Work, to labour Day and Night in it, that I may be the happy Inftrument of convincing Sinners, and edifying Saints, and faving Souls, and advancing the Gofpel of the Lord Jefus Chrift. And this I do in this turning time

of

of my Life ; befeeching God that
I may be found faithful, to his Glory, and to the eternal Advantage
of my own poor Soul, and the
Souls of many others Help O my
God, that I may abide herein to
my Lives end And when Time
fhall be no more, let me enjoy thee
for ever

To all which I put my Hand and
Seal, in the Prefence of the Great
God, Angels and Men.

T. B. ●

C H A P. VII.

Of my Temptations.

BUT altho' the Grace of God
hath thus happily difpos'd and
determin'd my Thoughts and Heart
for himfelf and Service ; yet I find
the Bufy Enemy ftill purfuing me,
trying to unhinge and unfettle
me. " Lord, come in to my Affi-
" ftance " O may I never hearken
to the Suggeftions of the evil one.
Lord

Lord help me, let not the E-
nemy prevail I know it is moſt
unreaſonable to yield, but I cannot
but fear, becauſe I find my own
corrupt Nature too apt to comply
with the Tempter ; without the
ſpecial Help of the good Spirit of
God, I may be yet overcome
God forbid " For the Lord Je-
" ſus Chriſt his Sake, help me, O
" my God

The Enemy would perſwade me
to deſiſt from Duty and Religion,
and to take my carnal Liberty.

But ſhall I apoſtatize from ſo
good a God, to ſerve ſuch a Slave?
Anſwer, O my Soul; Which is
beſt to ſerve, the God of Heaven,
or the God of this World ? Who
will reward me beſt ? If I ſerve
my God, I ſhall have Peace of
Conſcience, the Bleſſings of Providence, the Guidance and Comforts of the Spirit, the Enjoyment
of my God, and all the Happineſs
that is above, for ever and ever:
But if I ſerve the Enemy, he hath
nothing to give me ; he promiſeth
me great things, but there's nothing
with him but Torments, everlaſting

ing Torments; this is all the Reward he gives his Servants. A bad Paymaster indeed! Surely it is better being everlastingly happy than miserable. *Get thee behind me Satan.* O Lord my God, teach me, help me, that I may fly from him; that he may never be able to keep me from the Enjoyment of my Heavenly Father, and my dear Lord Jesus Christ for ever. *Amen.*

He suggests to me, That *it is Temp* 1. *Too soon; you are young, and have many Years before you: What need you to be busy?*

O cunning Enemy! Dost thou *Answ.* thus tempt me? Am I not the Son of good Parents? Was I not early devoted to the Service of the Great God? Do not I owe my first Fruits to my Maker? Is not my Childhood and Youth the Lord's? By the Help of the good Spirit of God, without whom I can do nothing, I am resolv'd to serve my God, in the Prime of my Days. Can I think he will take up with the Refuse of my Life; when I have serv'd the World, the Flesh and the Devil, with my Prime?

Can

Can I think he will accept of the
Blind and the Lame, when I have a
Lamb in the Flock? No, no. He
hath said, *Remember thy Creator in*
the Days of thy Youth , and why
should I defer longer? I find but
one Instance of late Repentance,
and why should I presume? This
I am sure of, if I serve my God in
the Prime of my Days, I shall find
Mercy, but if I defer longer, I am
altogether uncertain what may be
the Issue It is best being at Certain-
ties, in the great Concerns of ones Soul
and Eternity Shall I talk or think of
deferring, when I know not how
soon Death may be commission'd
by the great God to fetch me out
of this World, and bring me before
his great and awful Bar? And if it
should be before I am prepar'd to
meet him, how dreadful will my
Case be, and that for ever? Be
gore, thou Enemy of my Soul,
the Morning of my Age is the fit-
test time to begin the great Work,
and it may be the only Time I may
have; I will not, I am resolv'd, I
will not, thro' Grace, defer one
Moment.

But

But still I find the Enemy assault-*Temp.* 2
ing me *What then will you debar
your self of the Comforts and Pleasures
of this Life; and expose your self to all
manner of Troubles and Reproaches and
Sufferings, which your Religion is like
to cost you? If common Diversions
seem too mean, there are more noble and
delightful Delights; solace your self
with the Wit of the Age; let Plays and
Romances be your pleasing Study*

Oh what a Deceiver is my Ene-*Answ.*
my! What are all the Pleasures of
the World but poor and perishing?
What are these to a rational Soul?
How unsuitable and unmanly?
Shall I thus waste my Time, spend
my Estate, offend my good Friends,
provoke my God, and neglect my
Soul, and all to please the Flesh? I
will never do it It is only some
Shew of Pleasure, I have found it
real Bitterness My Pleasures have
cost me dear, for these I have o-
mitted Duty, adventur'd upon Sin;
I have indeed pleased the Flesh and
Satan, but have displeased God and
Conscience O! I would do so
no more What Pleasure can I
have in those things, whereof I am
no w

now aſhamed Senſual Pleaſures I
find a Sting to my Conſcience, a
Thorn in the Fleſh, Torments rather than Pleaſures I have met
with true and ſolid Comfort, and
Soul-ſatisfying Joy in the Way of
Duty and Religion ; which out-
weigh far all its Troubles and Difficulties There is nothing of Delight in the World comparable to
what I have found in the Enjoyment of God *One Hour's, yea one*
Moment's Communion with God, is
far beyond the ſenſual Delights of a
whole Life Shall I then leave the
Sweets and the Joys of the Holy
Ghoſt for the bitter Sweets of Sin,
which are but for a Moment, and
iſſue in everlaſting Torments?
Shall I loſe the Love of Jeſus, miſs
of Peace of Conſcience, rob my
ſelf of the Comforts of Life and
Death, and Eternity, which are
the Attendants of Religion ; and
all for brutal Delights, that may
make a Beaſt as happy as a Man?
Far be it from me. " O dear
" Lord Jeſus keep me, and keep up
" in me a Senſe of thy Love, and
" lively Affections, and Longings
" after

" after thy ſelf, and let me never be
" captivated by the poor and beg-
" garly Pleaſures of this Life *Amen*
" *and Amen* As for the Wit of the
World, I muſt confeſs it is very plea-
ſing and charming; but I find the
Wiſdom which is from above, is far
exceeding It is poor Satisfaction
that Plays and Romances afford
me, they are delightful whilſt I
read them, but they afford me no ſolid Comfort in the Review Lord,
thou kno veſt how uneaſy and tor-
menting it hath been to my Conſcience, I find they dreadfully
harden my Heart, and unfit me
for the Service of the great God,
and provoke the Spirit to withdraw The Reading of one hath
coſt me a thouſand Sighs and
Groans, and ſhall I venture further? No, no; I have better Books
to read, there is the holy Word of
God, the bleſſed and everlaſting
Goſpel, *a Book made in Heaven; a*
Book of my dear Redeemer's making;
a Book compoſed by the bleſſed Spirit;
the Book of Books; whilſt I read this,
I meet with ſolid Joy and Comfort
O Lord, let this be my Study,

D " my

" my Delight, my Meditation
" Day and Night Shall the Com-
pofures of profane Wits be prefer'd
before the Book of God? Satan,
fhould I delight more in thy Books
than in my Lord's? Hould bewitch-
ery! Get thee behind me, Satan

Temp 3. But he doth not yet depart; he
tells me, *Religion is not the Way ti*
Prefciment ; be wife and confide. thin
own Intereft

Anfw. I know it, I know it But it
the Way to everlafting Preferment
Godliaefs is great Gain, the greateft
Gain, if the Love of God, if an Intereft in Jefus, if Heaven, be fo
What Profit is it to gain a whole
World, and expofe my Soul for e-
ver? If I have God for my God
and Chrift for my Saviour, and the
Spirit for my Guide, and Heaven
for my End, I am fure I fhall not
want by the Way I have enough
and enough for ever and ever Sa
tan, fay no more I am above the
Temptation.

Temp. 4 But he will not let me alone,
he tells me, *You need not be fo ftrict*
you may adventure fometimes upon fmal
Sins : What is a little Lye, or *fuch*
fmal

small Matter, when it is for your In-
terest too ?

Shall I call any Sin small, that *Answ.*
is an Offence to my good God and
dear Redeemer ? Shall I adventure upon that which hath coſt me
ſo dear already ? One Sin once ruin'd Mankind, and what may ſeem
a little one too One Stab may de-
ſtroy my Life, and one Sin my
Soul One Sin may make Way for
more, eſpecially it preſumptuouſly
committed, and provoke the Grace
of God to withdraw, and then
where am I ? Sins of Infirmity are
like to be too numerous, and ſhall
I adventure upon wilful Commiſſi-
ons. The leaſt Sin deſerves eternal Torments, and ſhall I to gratify the wicked One run ſuch Ha-
zard ? Is a Lie nothing ? I'm ſure
it has coſt me Anguiſh enough. O
my Soul, look back, recollect that
Torment of Conſcience, thoſe
Fears and Dangers, that little Sins,
even a Lie have expos'd me to How
ſhall I anſwer for theſe at the Bar
of a juſt God ? Shall I thus drudge
and ſlave my ſelf to the Enemy ?
O horrid ! I have had enough, I
have

have had too much of Sin " The " Lord give me Grace that I may " not touch the accursed Thing Satan, be gone.

Temp. 5. But he hath other Devices He *disswades me from a constant Attendance upon Duty What need you be so strict? What need you pray so oft, and read so much? It will weary the Flesh, and tire the Spirits, and run up Religion into Superstition Be not righteous over much*

Answ. And shall I dare to omit any known Duty! It hath cost me dear already, and shall I adventure again? The Lord knows what Pleasure I have found in his Service: O how sweet hath Duty been, hath Prayer been to me! *I remember his Love more than Wine.* I have been guilty of too many Neglects, and shall I make the Breach worse? God forbid One Omission may wrong my Soul, provoke my God, and quench the Spirit, and let in the Tempter upon me. " The " Lord make me more wise, and " wise for eternal Salvation, Satan be gone, this will not, this shall never do.

But

But he purfues ftill. *You may Temp.*
give your felf Allowances at the prefent,
and return afterwards to your Duty
you may enjoy the Comforts of both
Worlds. Take a Loofe, and try what
good things the World hath, and then
turn at length, I do not diffwade you
from Religion, but perfwade you to tafte
the Sweets of the Creatures in your
Minority, and when more ripe and fit
for Religion, then to engage in it.

O cunning Enemy! Shall I de- *Anfw*
nift from Religion, with a Defign
and Purpofe of returning to God
again? *No, I will not.* How can
I promife my felf Grace to do this,
and Acceptance with God. Shall
I quench the Motions of the Spirit
now, what Affurance can I have
that he will ever return again? If
I put off God now, may he not juft-
ly leave me to my felf When fhall
I return again? it will be too late
when in the Grave; there I am
fure will be no Room for Repentance, and whilft I give the Flefh
its Liberty, Death may feize me.
I may hear, who knows, *This*
Night fhall thy Soul be required It
will be too late to return, when
D 3 under

under the Seizures, and in the Clutches of the Enemy. Will he let me go I dare not venture him, tho' it may not be impoffib'e to return afterwards, it is very unlikely and exceeding dangerous I charge thee therefore, O my Soul, not to dare to apoftatize the leaft from God, which thou haft feen and felt the evil Effects of already. O horrid Impiety! O unreafonable Demands! What leave fo good a God! What, flave for fuch a fworn and defperate Enemy!

By the Help of the bleffed Spirit of God I will not defer one Moment. I cannot fay, I have not been called in my Youth; for God's good Spirit inclines me now, and now if I engage with God, I am fure of Mercy; if I refufe, I muft be inexcufable. I will not dare to fin wilfully any more, nor neglect a known Duty. I will never think of returning afterwards These are all the Cheats of the reftlefs and fubtle Enemy Now without Delay, I will fubmit to God, and feek an Intereft in Chrift, in his Sufferings, Crucifixion, Death and Refurrection.

furrection, and Interceffion; To whom be Kingdoms, Power and Glory for ever, *Amen*

Satan, be gone, fay no more; I am refolv'd

O that all this I have wrote and done, may not be as a Witnefs againft me. O my Soul, be yet more concern'd, it is wifeft working whilft our Day lafteth. Now's the **Time**, I am a poor mortal Creature, in **Danger of Death**

O that I was but more fit to ftand before the Bar of a juft God. 'Tis time to work, Death is abroad A dangerous Fever about; and Sicknefs already is broke into the Family. Lord help· Let this effectual- ly draw me to thy felf, *Amen.*

D 4 CHAP.

C H A P. VIII.

Of his Death.

THIS is the *Legacy* our dear Deceafed Friend hath left us, which to me is far better than Silver or Gold: Becaufe a good Evidence of his early Piety and Sincerity in this World, and his eternal Happinefs in the other.

The Sicknefs he fpeaks of in the Family, I fuppofe was (tho' very flightly upon others) the Fiery Chariot and Horfes, that conveyed him fafe home to his heavenly Father. *What is but an Infirmity to one may prove Death to another.* He wifely took the firft Allarm It is heavenly Wifdom indeed, fo to number our Days, as to take the firft Item of Danger, and engage our Hearts in the main Work *Blefed is he,* the Old, the Young, *whom his Lord when he cometh fhall find fo doing*, for who knows but a very Spark may foon be blown up into a mighty, yea, an unquenchable Flame. Often

ten the firft Approaches of Death
aie filent and calm, when its after
Suzures are more violent and pref-
fing · And either fink us under In-
capacities, or doze us with Inob-
fervance Which was the Cafe of
this Ho'y Youth

His Diftemper began in its low-
eft Degrees, and advanc'd fome
Days fo flowly, that no Danger
appear'd, which yet in about a
Weeks Space confin'd him to his
Chamber · Where the Body was
imprifon'd, but the Soul ftill at
Liberty All was bore with that
Patience, as if it had been but the
Shadow of a Diftemper; and private Duty ftill carried on, which
nothing but an utter Inability
could fuperfede

About three Days after his Con-
finement, a fevere Fever Fit feiz'd
him, which ftruck deep upon his
Spirits, tho' ftill the Phifician ap-
prehended no Danger, neither did
he himfelf It pleafeth God often
to hide from Friends and Phificians,
and our felves too, the Changes
his Providence is introducing
And all this in very great Mercy

D 5   too,

too, to Souls duly prepar'd for his
coming   The Fears of Death are
worfe to the Righteous than Death
it felf   It is fome Mercy to Die,
and not feel the Sting of Death
An unfeen Blow tho' Mortal is not
frightful

Nature was much fpent by this
fevere and fiery Tryal, yet ftill
Grace inclined to Duty   Prayer
was not omitted   *It is good to live,*
and die praying,   After this Storm,
there was fome hopeful Calm,
which reviv'd our finking Hopes
But the next Day he was feiz'd
with another Fit, that bore down
all our Hopes, that with a ftrange
inward Fury dry'd up his Spirits,
and wafted all before it. Yet that
Evening he would be led to his
Bed-fide, that upon his bended
Knees he might once more addrefs
Heaven, tho' he could neither bow
the Knee alone, nor arife without
Help

Thus he finifhed his ftated Attendances, and betook himfelf to his
laft Bed. But tho' a Fire within
wafted like a Houfe in Flames, yet
as meek as a Lamb, he made no
Outcry of Danger.   **The**

The next Morning, Death came on very vifibly to all about him, tho' ftill imperceptible to himfelf. He had the free Exercife of Reafon, tho' under great Dulnefs, the Strength of Nature being much exhaufted

I found him well fatisfy'd as to the State of his Soul; not indeed lifted up with peremptory Confidence, but modeftly Hoping, Repenting, Praying, Believing *A very good Frame fure, either to live or die in.* I told him, I was afraid we fhould lofe him He anfwer'd, he hop'd not yet So willing was he to do his Mafter fome Services I told him, he did not defire my Remembrances O I do, faith he, tho' I don't fpeak much, be pleas'd to pray for me

I fpake to him of his Relations, he faid he fhould be glad to fee them, but was eafy without. *He that hath fecur'd the beft Friends in Heaven, may be fatisfied in the Abfence of the beft Relations on Earth.* His dear Grandfather was upon the Road to fee him, but found a dead Child, who I doubt not hath fince
found

found him in a better World, having return'd and finish'd his Course, which he had fill'd up with as much private Devotion as any one Candidate for Heaven. Alass! Two Praying Friends quickly lost! And *Praying Friends are some of the best Friends.*

I inquired of him as to his Estate, what he was pleased to do, and found him desirous all should run on, without any Alteration, into his Dear Brother's Possession, whose Welfare here and for ever, he had very much at Heart.

Some of his Companions in the Evening, designing once more to retire, and unite their Prayers for him; one of them ask'd him, what he desir'd particularly they should request for him, he answer'd, *That he might be more useful*; and so he is now. For how low, and dull, and mean, are our Services, at the Footstool of Grace, in comparison of theirs that are before the Throne of Glory. Ours are Deadness, theirs are Life : Ours are Shadows, theirs are Substance : Ours are Wishes, theirs are Performances:
Ours

Ours are Earth, theirs are Heaven

Still the precious Soul apprehen-
ded not its Removal. It is un-
speakable Happiness to be before-
hand with Death There's no
Danger in dying, tho' we fee not
the Blow given, when Soul and All
is before fecured in the Hands
of a Redeemer.

In the closing Devotions of the
Day, when the whole Family was
conven'd together, as we were
commending him to the Grace of
God, and intreating that the tri-
umphant Convoy might be ready
to mount upon their Wings the
gracious departing Soul, but with
interrupted Expreffions, every Eye
weeping, and every Heart bleed-
ing, being all concern'd to part
with one univerfally beloved;
whilft we were thus refigning him
into the Arms of Divine Love; the
over-hafty Soul took its Flight from
us, juft as his holy Father's did; to
ufe the Expreffions of a very worthy Perfon to me, *He went off with
a Gale of Prayer. We loft as much in
him, as could be loft in one Man* I
may

may fay the very fame concerning
the Holy Seed. *He went up in the*
Cloud of Incenfe. In the Lofs of whom,
we loft all that could be loft in one Ho-
ly Branch

Thus was he furpriz'd into Glory, and died as it were without dying   Death privately conquering
it felf   Whilft he thought himfelf
on Earth, among his old Friends,
he found himfelf in Heaven, a-
mong his glorified Relations, and
with his moft glorious Redeemer
Whilft he was thinking of better
Service here, he found himfelf engag'd in perfect Adorations Above,
and for ever

Oh Glorious Exchange ! Agreeable
Surprize ! Blessed Eternity !

The Holy Seed :

O R, A

FUNERAL DISCOURSE

Occasion'd by the Death of

Mr. *Thomas Beard.*

Sept. 15. 1710.

PSALM xxii. xxx.

A Seed shall serve him, it shall be accounted to the Lord for a Generation.

I Am called forth this Day to *hard Service*, to *very hard Service* ; to preach a Funeral Sermon for one of my own Family, planted here as my own from his In-

Infancy. I muſt acknowledge it to the Praiſe of the Goodneſs of God, that this is the firſt Life I have loſt in near Thirty Years Attendance upon the Education of Youth; and a very precious and valuable Life is loſt, it is ſo in it ſelf, and more abundantly to Me A *Religious* Branch of a Religious Family is cut off: A gracious Branch of *Glorify'd* Parents is returned to the Root; of whom I have often thought and ſaid, " When I am ſilenc'd in the Duſt, " and ſhall ſpeak no more in the " Name of the Lord, he will ariſe, " and be the Lord's Meſſenger, " and a skilful and acceptable one Of whom all that knew him have been ready to ſay, *This* is the Seed of the Righteous, that is riſing up to ſerve the Lord Jeſus · But by a ſurprizing Stroke he is commanded home · A Seed prepar'd on Earth to ſerve his Lord in a better Place. Little did I think of doing this Service for him, of whom I might rather have expected it; but we only gueſs like poor fallible Men. Alas! our hopes are cut off, they *are gone*
down

d;wn *to the Bars of the Pit* (as *Job*
fpeaketh) *they reft together in the Duft*
But it is ftill a Seed to ferve the
Lord, tho' not in this Generation,
yet in a more glorious Station

A Seed fhall ferve him

This is an *Evangelick* Pfalm, as
is manifeft by feveral Paffages in it:
Wherein we have an Account of the
Sufferings of Chrift, and the Glorious Iffue and Effect thereof; that
he fhall have a Seed to ferve him,
both *Jews* and *Gentiles* fhall be con-
verted to him. The Evangelick
Pfalmift fpeaks of the Jews, and
their Seed: *Praife him all the Seed of* Ver. 23.
Jacob, *and fear him all the Seed of*
Ifrael. You and Yours fubmit to
the *Meffiah.* He fpeaks alfo of the
Gentile Believers, and their Seed:
All the Ends of the Earth fhall re- Ver 27
member, and turn unto the Lord, and
all the Kindreds of the Nations
worfhip before thee &c. and then
adds, *A Seed fhall ferve him, it fhall*
be accounted to the Lord for a Genera-
tion, i e The Lord Jefus Chrift
fhall have a Seed that fhall ferve
him, and this Seed fhall be moftly
rais'd

rais'd out of *Religious Gentile Fami-lies*, and continued in all Genera-tions, which are the Doctrinal Truths of this Verse: The Subjects of Christ's Kingdom are chiefly the Gentile Believers and their Poste-rity. Their Work and Duty is to serve the Lord Jesus, then Honour and Happiness is, that they are de-signed to be the Instruments of transmitting Religion to the Gene-rations to come.

Here then we must consider,

I. *That the Lord Jesus Christ shall have a Seed.*

II. *That this Seed shall serve him.*

III *That this Seed that shall serve the Lord, shall be raised mostly from the Posterity of Gentile Believers*

IV *That there shall be a Succession of such Seed in all Generations*

I *Gen* The Lord Jesus Christ hath had in all Ages, and shall have *a Seed*. This is a very com-fortable Truth, the Gates of Hell cannot prevail; if some are cut off from the Land of the Living, o-thers shall arise to serve the Lord Jesus

Jesus *Of Zion it shall be said,* this Psal 87 5.
and that Man was born in her All
Ages shall produce some serious
holy believers, *and the Highest himself shall establish her,* the Almighty
will secure a gracious Succession.
For,

1 The Father hath promised,
and given to the Son a Seed to serve
him He came into the World with
this Assurance from infinite Truth
and Love, *That he should see his Seed,* Isa. 53. 11.
*the Travil of his Soul, and be satis-
fied, and divide the Spoil with the
Strong* This was the Original
Contract betwixt the Father and
the Son, upon his undertaking the
great and glorious Work of Redemption "My dear Son, if thou
" wilt interpose, and make up the
' Breach between me and the poor
" Sinner, by pouring out thy Soul
' into Death Believe me, thou
" shalt not lose thy Labour, I give
" thee, I promise thee a Seed to
" full Content, I give thee my
" Divine Word and Assurance for
" it · Some thou shalt be certain of
" as a Seed to serve thee in all A-
" ges to the End of the World
A

A Bleſſed Covenant! An Elect
Seed! Eternally happy Souls that
are of this number

The Father of Mercies will never deceive his dear Son; he is
faithful, and will exactly fulfil his
Promiſe The Lord Jeſus Chriſt
ſo prizeth the Father's Gift, that
he will not loſe any Part of it He
ſpeaks of this with great Admira-
Heb. 2. 13. tion: *Behold, I and the Children that*
God hath given me! Amazing Grace!
That amidſt the fiery Oppoſition
that is made to Chriſt, and the
Chriſtian Religion, any ſhould be
born to him; but the Pleaſure of
the Lord, which is the Pleaſure of
his Soul, ſhall proſper in his Hands
With what Delight hath he ex-
Joh. 6. 37 preſs'd himſelf: *All that the Father*
hath given me, ſhall come to me, and
him that cometh to me I will in no
wiſe caſt out; q d. I am perſwaded
that my Father will raiſe me a Seed,
as he hath aſſured me: And I am
reſolved with the greateſt Concern
to regard and preſerve my Father's
Gift. By no means in the World
ſhall they be neglected. For indeed,

2. The

2. The Son himſelf hath dearly purchaſed a Seed to ſerve him He travail'd with Death to bring forth a Chriſtian Seed : What Pangs and Throws, and Agonies, did he undergo to bring forth living Children? The Father hath given his dear Son a Seed, but he muſt firſt redeem them to himſelf from the Grave and Hell · He muſt reſcue them out of the Hand of the Deſtroyer, which he hath effected by a mighty and bloody Victory over all the Powers of Darkneſs Having accompliſh'd this, he is gone to Heaven to make his Claim, which we find he began on Earth. ' Righteous Father, fulfil now thy ' Promiſe to thine own dear Son, ' who hath finiſh'd my Work. I ' now with Submiſſion demand a ' Seed on Earth to ſerve me ; and ' 'tis my Will they ſhould ſee my ' Glory too : Holy Father, I ' commend them all to thine infi- ' nite Grace.

John 17

3 The Father and Son have put it into the Hands of the bleſſed Spirit, to prepare this Seed ; and whilſt that Infinite and Almighty Spirit
hath

hath the Management, the Seed cannot fail Satan cannot hinder it, he must *fall as Lightning* before him. He will easily *divide a Portion with the Strong*, for who can resist an Infinite Deity. The Work is not left to the lubricous corrupt Will of Man, nor to the Weakness of Ministers, 'tis put into better Hands, into the Hands of the Son and the Spirit " Son, look to thy " Seed thy self, and let the eternal " Spirit serve under thee. Thus their Names are wrote in the *Lamb's Book of Life before the Foundation of the World* Thus the Holy Seed is secur'd, being the Gift and Charge of the Father; the Purchase and Charge of the Son; the Work and Charge of the Spirit.

This is the Seed.

II *Gen* This Seed shall serve the Lord Jesus Christ, they are promis'd, purchas'd, rais'd, design'd, and prepar'd for this Service. To serve Christ, is to attend on him in the Solemnities of his Worship, and to advance his Glory and Interest in our several Places and Relations, and

and all from fanctify'd Principles.
The great Springs of Devotion are
active Love, filial Fear, Faith un-
feigned, and a firm Reliance on
the Grace of Chrift; *Amor meus
pond* meum*, &c. By thefe the
chofen Seed are mov'd in their
Sphere of Duty I fhall therefore
confider, in their Scriptural and ef-
fential Characters, their gracious
Conftitution, and then their fpiritual Operations in their full Extent
and Scope

1 The Characters of the Chofen Seed we meet with in Scripture,
are fuch as thefe ; They are a *holy,
godly Seed, a good, right, Chriftian
Seed*, and a *praying chofen Seed*: Very glorious *Titles*, and gracious
Characters

They are called the *holy Seed :* Ifa 6 13.
A very Divine Character Holy
they fhould be, as their Lord is
holy; their Hearts, their Lives,
their Duties, their Relations holy.
All holy, holy in all manner
of Converfation and Godlinefs
This Holy Seed is the *Subftance* of
the Church of God As the Sap
and Spirits are the very Life of the
Tree,

Tree, hence it springs and flourish-
eth, hence is its Growth and Con-
tinuance. When it fails, it withers
1 Cor. 7 and dies Thus are their *Children*
14. *holy*

Matt. 13 2. They are called the *good Seed.*
24. A very sweet and pleasant Name
A Seed free from prevailing Cor-
ruptions, fit for Production and In-
crease, for present and for future
Supply, the very Hope of a full
Crop and plentiful Harvest. The
chosen Seed should be of a very *tender* and *merciful* Disposition, whose
Ambition and Aim should be to *be
good* and *do good*, and thus transmit
Goodness yet *further* with good In-
crease.

Mal. 2. 15. They are called the *Godly Seed*
A Noble, Excellent, Godlike Seed,
of God and for God, raised by the
Power of God, to promote Godliness, and to continue a godly Seed
in the World, whose Care must be
to live to God, and to die to God,
that whether living or dying, they
may be the Lord's, and leave behind them not a spurious, but a
godly Posterity.

They

They are called a *Right Seed*, Je 2. 2
'Jolly a right Seed, upright in
themselves, and prepared for the
Propagation of an upright Generation Their Hearts right and
their Services so. No Cheats nor
Pretenders. *Ifraelites indeed, in
whom there is no Guile*; noble Plants,
that give a fair Profpect of a Holy
Posterity. Tho' too many prov'd
degenerate ones, who instead of
propagating Religion, propagated
Vice, and Immorality, and Idola-
try Ten thoufand Pities!

They are reprefented as a *Chu*—Heb 2.
fen Seed, the Likenefs of their
Lord, as Children the Likenefs of
their Parents, Partakers of the Nature and Temper of the holy Jefus,
and conformed to his holy Life
Thefe are the Children of the
Kingdom, the Gofpel Kingdom,
defigned for Promoters and Prote-
ctors of it

They are reprefented as a *Pray-*
ing Seed Prayer is the natural
Language of the fpiritual Seed
Abba, Father, are the firft Words
they learn to fpeak *This is the Gofpel's*
Notion of them that feek thee And the

E   Seed

Seed of *Jacob* shall not seek in vain.

1 Pet. 2. 9. *Lastly*, A *Chosen Seed* ; chosen of God, as *Jacob* of old, *the Children of* Jacob *his chosen* ; chosen through Grace to serve the Lord, and to propagate a Seed to serve him.

2. Which Seed is called forth to serve the Lord Jesus in their private Capacities, in their Generation, in the Church of God, and some in the Ministry This is the Sphere in which they are appointed to move. Their Service begins,

1 *In their private Capacities.* This implies personal Devotion, and a truly Christian Conversation. 'Tis never right till the way to our Closets is as a beaten Road, and our daily Walk 'Tis never right till it may be said of our Houses, the Church of God in their House. And how much will a regular Life, that is a Transcript of Christ's own, adorn a Religious Closet and Family ? Whereas a looser Conversation belies all the personal Devotion

The Holy Seed are appointed to maintain personal, in order to Family Religion ; without the former,

mer, the latter muſt neceſſarily drop, and both in order to ſupport it

2 *In their Generation.* Which implies their fixing in ſome lawful Calling, and advancing the Intereſt of Chriſt, whatever in them lies, in the World. We may ſerve Chriſt in any lawful Calling, if we are prudent, careful, and holy therein, and ſome ſuch Calling all ſhould apply themſelves to, and abide therein, according to the Advice of the Apoſtle. Where 'tis for ever determined, that the Chriſtian Religion doth not diſpenſe with an idle unprofitable Life, which muſt be a Diſparagement to Religion it ſelf, but commands a conſtant Attendance in ſome honeſt Vocation, wherein we muſt labour to advance the Truth, and Power, and Glory of Chriſtianity, ſerving God and our Generation. Thus ſhould the Holy Seed ariſe and build. As the Prophet predicts, *Thoſe that come of Jacob ſhould take root, and bloſſom and bud, and fill the Face of the Earth with Fruit* To promote this it is neceſſary to fix themſelves,

1 Cor. 7. 20.

Iſa. 27. 6

E 2 3. *In*

3. *In the Church of God.* By a constant Attendance upon all the Ordinances there, and incorporating themselves as Members with some Religious Society Our Saviour hath given us his Example, and the Spirit of God hath given us an Account of the Primitive Converts; that they were added to the Church, and continued in Prayer together, and in other Gospel Ordinances Thus the Philosopher directs, *υπ α μ· · · π·· ·* Publick Attendances are the chiefest These mostly resemble Heaven, that *General Assembly* These most promote the Honour of God, and the Interest of Religion in the World . Christ is glorify'd, when his Word is carefuly heard, when his Sabbaths are religiously observed, when his Sacraments are duly and constantly attended, and the solemn Assembly frequented The Lord Jesus Christ is flighted when his Institutions are slighted; he is opposed when his Ordinances are opposed The Glory the Father expects through Christ, according to the Apostle, is from, and in the *Church.*   This

This is foretold concerning the Holy Seed, *That from one Sabbath to* Isa. 66 2 *another, they shall come and worship before the Lord in his holy Mount,* i. e. in a fixed stated manner shall bring their Offerings unto the Lord *in a set in Vessel* Thus all Governments are maintain'd and promoted in mixed Societies The very Nature or the thing requires this of the chosen Seed, as they desire to plant the Gospel, and propagate a Gospel Religion Hence 'tis necessary that some of the hopeful and godly Seed should serve the Lord Jesus.

4 *In the Ministry.* For what Society can subsist without stated Officers? It would be a strange Family without a Head; a strange Government without a Governour, a strange Kingdom and no Ruler, a strange Flock and no Shepherd God hath appointed his Officers out of the Promised Seed This was foretold, *Isa* 61. 5 *The Gentile Strangers shall feed their Flocks, and the Sons of the Alien shall be their Plowmen and Vinedressers;* which is explained, Chap 66 21. *I will take of them for Priests and for Levites,*

E 3 *faith*

faith the Lord. To ferve God in the Miniftry is the higheft and hardeft Piece of Service It is to be *Embaffadors* of *Chrift*, and *Fellow-laboureus* with Angels, to be *Stars* in the Right Hand of Chrift · This is great Honour, but it requires double Service, that of private Chriftians, and that of publick Officers, who of all are moft expofed to Apoftate Spirits, and the Scorn of finful Men : But the double Honour of this, and the eternal World fwallow up all the Difficulties and Troubles of the Miniftry.

This is the Work of the chofen Seed

III *Gen* This Seed is defigned to be chiefly and mainly rais'd out of the Pofterity of the Righteous This is very comfortable, and muft be a very pleafing Doctrine to Religious Parents, who have moft at Heart the fpiritual Welfare and eternal Happinefs of theirs ; to be Inftruments of raifing up a Seed for Chrift, and to prepare a Seed for Heaven, is high Honour now, and will be a Crown of Glory at laft Happy, happy Parents, whofe Families

milies are Chrift's, and whofe Children are God's own, *Whofe Seed fhall be accounted to the Lord for a Generation.*

1 This is the more general Interpretation of the Text, and that of the moft Learned Expofitors. *Pofteritas Credentium eorum Pofteri:* Their Seed fhall ferve him ; and this feems the moft natural Senfe of the Words. The Pfalmift in the precedent Verfes is fpeaking of Gentile Believers, and adds, a *Seed* fhall ferve him If it be demanded what Seed ? Whofe Seed ? The direct Anfwer is, the Seed of the Gentile Believers, of whom he was fpeaking, as he was of the Jews, and their Seed ; *q. d* " The Jews and their Ver.13. " Seed called and chofen of God " for a Generation above all Peo- " ple to bear the Name of God, I " forefee will fail thro' their Un- Deut. 1 " belief : But the Meffiah fhall not 25. " want a Seed ; for in the room of " the Jews and their Seed, the " Gentiles fhall arife, and their " Seed, who fhall be accounted to " the Lord for a Generation Out " of thefe God will raife his Church " moftly. E 4 2. This

2 This Interpretation suits exactly with other Scripture Promises *One Text of Scripture best explains another.* In many other Places where the Seed is spoke of, that shall arise and serve the Lord, 'tis plainly meant of the Seed of the Gentile Believers This therefore according to the Analogy of Faith, seems the most genuine Sense of the Psalmist I shall quote a few Places both in the Old and New Testament, which give Light to this Text 'Tis said, speaking of the Gentiles, *They are the Seed of the Blessed of the Lord, and their Offspring with them,* i e. their Children Blessed Parents and

... to the Gentiles to believe in the ... that God would make with them ...

fure

sure as *David* and his Seed had the
Throne of *Israel* ascertained to
them, from Generation to Generation, unless by their wilful Apo-
stacy from God, they cut off the
Entail. So certainly would a gracious God own the Believing Gentiles, as well as *Jews*, and their Seed
for ever, unless by their Unbelief
they prevented themselves All
which seems confirm'd, *The Promise* Acts 2 39
to you and your Children, and to as
many as the Lord our God shall call,
to the Gentiles equally as to
th Jews *Abraham*'s natural Seed,
and *Abraham*'s Spiritual Seed, are
both to be accounted to the Lord
for a Generation The Golden
Line of Grace shall run on As the
God of *Abraham*, *Isaac* and *Jacob*
So the God of Gospel Believers,
and their Seed and Seed's Seed

3. This Explication suits with
the Dispensations of the Grace of
God in all Ages The Seed of the
Righteous have been the Seed of
the Church, in the Time of *Adam*,
Noah, *Abraham* and the *Jews* And
the Gentile Believers are frequently express'd by the Names of *Israel*

and

and *Jacob,* therefore as the Jewiſh, ſo the Goſpel Church muſt be moſtly maintain'd by Believer's Poſterity

4 This Interpretation agrees exactly with that Repreſentation of the Church of God we have in Scripture. It is called a Kingdom, a Family, now 'tis the Children in both that are the main Supports of both: Theſe are the Hopes of Kingdoms and Families ; thus they are propagated, if theſe fail, Kingdoms and Families muſt quickly fall too The Gentile Believers 1 Pet. 2 9 are call'd *a choſen Generation, and a holy Nation,* as the Jews were, whoſe Children were the Support of their Nation, and the propagatory Seed of the Church

5 And to conclude, The Experience of all Chriſtians clearly evidenceth this Truth Pray, how is the Church of God moſtly maintain'd ; is it not raiſed out of Religious Families ? Tell me how it hath been in your Days ? The Diſpenſations of Grace in the Church of God, are good Interpreters of the Promiſes of Grace

made

made to the Church of God. *The Operations of Grace are answerable to the Promises of Grace* Must not that be the meaning of the Promise, which is the daily Work of the Spirit of God? If the Church of God be generally maintain'd by the Offspring of Believers, it must be their Offspring that is intended in those Promises, that speak of a Seed to serve the Lord.

Neither is there any thing objected against this Doctrine as I know of, which is of any great Force

Whereas it may be said, *That ma-* *ny of the Children of good Parents prove loose and profligate* It must be own'd it is no strange thing for an *Esau* to sell his *Birthright*. There are too too many degenerate Plants: This is a very sorrowful Truth, and what is most shameful; it is ten thousand Pities it should be so; And I must pronounce *Woe to the Apostates in religious Families.* It will be more tolerable for *Sodom* and *Comorrah,* and the Children of Infidels in the Day of Judgment, than for such The *Children of the Kingdom* that are degenerate will be

Obj. 1

sentenc'd

sentenc'd to *Outward Darkness* But this hinders not that the Church of God is mostly raised out of the Posterity of the Righteous What if some Children prove undutiful, and are disinherited; prove prodigal and waste their Inheritance, doth it hence follow, that Children are not the Props and Supports of Families? What if some Subjects are rebellious, and forfeit their Birthright, and are banish'd their Native Country, doth it follow that Kingdoms are not generally maintain'd by the free born Seed? And do not even adult Professors very often apostatize? and yet the Church of God is supported by the Professors of it

Obj 2. And whereas it may be said, That this Doctrine of peculiar Grace to the Posterity of the Righteous, *exposeth the greater Part of the World to Ruin.* This is a very unjust Inference It hath been already said, That when the Free Grace of God lays hold on alien Families, they and theirs are accounted for a Generation; though mostly the Church of God is promoted by the
Posterity

Posterity of the Righteous. And that others are not added, who is in the Fault? when they have the Liberty, and free Offer to incorporate themselves and theirs in this happy Society, this holy Family and Kingdom. Is there any other Government in the World so free, to offer a general Naturalization to all, upon their Submission to the known Laws thereof? The Gospel contains an universal Invitation, and assures of an universal Welcome to all who by Faith unite with the Church of God, tho' there is somewhat peculiar propos'd to believing Families, who have the first Offers of Grace, whose Lot is cast at the very Gates of Salvation. And yet as the *Jews* did, they too often put Salvation from them.

What therefore hath been pleaded for, remains a well-grounded Truth.

That the Father hath promised the Son a Seed to serve him; that the Lord Jesus Christ hath died and purchased this Seed, that the Advancement thereof is intrusted in the Hands of the Blessed Spirit; which

which Seed, according to promife, is to be rais'd moftly out of the Pofterity of the Righteous ; and not by a new Acceffion of alien Families : But yet when the free Grace of God lays hold on any of thefe, they and theirs fhall be accounted to the Lord for a Generation And the Defection of fome of the Holy Seed, can ro ways contradict this Doctrine, which allows them the firft Offers of Grace, and afferts that thus ordinarily the Church of God is maintain'd.

IV *Gen.* And thus laftly, The Church of God fhall be maintain'd in all Generations Not for a few Years or Ages, but to the very end of Time. The Seed that is defign'd for the Service of Chrift, and given to him of the Father, is to be gather'd out of all Ages As appears from the facred Records, as, *Inftead of thy Fathers fhall be thy Children,* i c. Inftead of Fathers which are thine, fhall be their Children which fhall be thine too And thus I will make thy Name to be remembred in all Generations. There's a glorious Prophecy in *I-faiah,*

Pfal. 45. v. 16, 17.

ſaiah, As for me, this is my Covenant, a Gracious Evangelical Covenant. *My Spirit which is upon* Iſa. 49.
thee, and my Words that I have put in
thy Mouth, ſhall not depart out of thy
Mouth, nor out of the Mouth of thy
S d, nor out of the Mouth of thy Seed's
Seed, ſaith the Lord, from henceforth
and for ever A Promiſe worthy to
be wrote on every Heart, and to
be the Motto of every Religious
Family. Let the Seed, and the
Seed's Seed, learn it perfectly
Let Miniſters, Parents and Children, ſtudy this mighty Word of
Grace. The Lord Jeſus Chriſt
ſhall have a Seed in all Ages This
was the Original Covenant. Thus
'twas ſettled by the Father and the
Son

And indeed,

1. The Lord Jeſus is worthy of
a Seed in all Ages. It would be
too little Glory to have his Seed
confin'd to one or a few Ages.
He deſerves an Eternity of Service,
and ſurely then that of Time If
all in every Age were true to Chriſt,
it would be beneath his Merits.
The leaſt that can be thought of is
ſome

some in every Age; that when one Generation goes off, another may arise to serve him And there shall not be one Age to the End of Time, so dark, so virulent, that the Glory of Christ shall be altogether eclipsed *Christ hath redeemed to God by his Blood, out of every Tongue and People, and Nation, those that should ascribe Blessing and Honour, and Glory, and Power to the Lamb for ever and ever, for he is worthy, &c*

2 Such a continued Succession of a Seed to serve Christ, tends mostly to the Glory of Divine Wisdom and Grace All Ages need a Saviour, all Ages therefore shall have the Offer, and whilst there's a Certainty of some good Effect, 'tis more honourably offer'd to all It would be below the Majesty, and Wisdom, and Grace of God, by stated Officers, to publish the Overture of Mercy to the World, if all would be certainly ineffectual. Were there not some to be gather'd out of every Age, there would want some to balance the World, even a Blessing in it, for whose sake it should not be destroy'd.

troy'd But for the fake of thefe
he wicked World is honourably
,,,,d, and Judgments fuperfeded,
without which Divine Juftice would
quickly proceed to Execution For
the Elect fake Judgments are over-
ruled, and the Day of Judgment
defer'd, and the Patience of God
appears in Glory; but when all
thefe fhall be gather'd in from one Matth.24
End of the World to the other, then 31.
Judgment commenceth, and till
then every Age will afford a Seed
to ferve our Lord, which fhall be
accounted unto him for a Generation

From what hath been faid, we
may infer,

1 That *the Lord Jefus Chrift is
God* He that is to be ferved in all
Generations, and hath a holy Seed
appointed on purpofe for Religious
Service and Adoration, to whom
Princes themfelves muft pay Ho-
mage, muft needs be God Yea,
Angels too muft Worfhip him, and
all muft honour him as they honour the Father As no Creature
is, fo the human Nature of Chrift
cannot be adorable, and therefore
he

he muſt have a Divine Nature
The Godhead is in it ſelf adorable,
and the Perſon of the Son, by rea-
ſon of his Divine Nature is aoora-
ble, yea, the Divine Perſon of the
Son, in our Nature too is adorable
Woiſhip him all ye Angels. Let the
choſen Seed ſerve him.

II. That *the Election the Goſpel
ſpeaks of, is not meerly of Qualifica-
tions, but of Perſons.* 'Tis true God
hath choſe Faith in Chriſt, as the
neceſſary Qualification in all thoſe
he will own, and ſave for ever and
ever. But he hath likewiſe choſe
ſome whom he will thus accompliſh
Eph. 1. 4. for his Service and Glory, *As he hath
choſen us in him before the Foundation
of the World, that we ſhould be holy,
and without blame before him in Love.*
He doth not only in Time chooſe
ſome of the number of Sinners, but
there is a Seed promis'd and given
to Chriſt, before the World, to be
prepar'd to ſerve him . The Lord
Jeſus Chriſt was at certainty as to
a Seed ; and the whole Effect of
Redemption was not left to turn
upon the lubricous, fallacious and
corrupt Will of Man. There was

a certain Seed chofe to be qualified according to the Gofpel, and not meerly becaufe God did forefee they would be thus qualified This is that *Number of the Elect which God will portly accomplifh.*

III Hence it follows further, that *Religion hath its peculiar Excellacies and Encouragements* 'Tis ftrange that Religion fhould fall under Difreputation, which entails fo many Bleffings upon Pofterity, to the utmoft Date thereof. Is there any Government in the World, that fecures to the Seed of its Favourites a Perpetuity, nay an Eternity of Bleffings? Eftates, and Honours, that Men venture their Names, their Lives and Souls to engrofs, are attended with Thoufands of Uncertainties ; whilft Religion fixeth fuch an Entail of Mercy, that nothing but the Profligatenefs of Pofterity can reverfe. A Gracious God gives you leave to put your own Names, and the Names of yours, in a Leafe of Grace, in which the Bleffings of Time and Eternity are well fettled, as an everlafting Inheritance from

Gene-

Generation to Generation Who P
would refuse such an Offer? If the t
World should propose any Thing C
like it, what Shift would there be n
for the Predicament? O let Reli-e
gion be your Business, which is F
moſt excellent in it ſelf, and entails
Bleſſings to the laſt Duration of it
If you love your ſelves, or regard
Poſterity, take heed to your ſelves
and yours. Which teacheth us further,

IV That *the Work and Duty of
religious Parents and Miniſters is very
great.* They are to take Care of the
Holy Seed that is deſigned for the
Service of our dear Lord Jeſus, to
feed the Lambs It is a great Truſt
that is committed to their Charge:
The *Soul's* of Children, and what
more valuable? Your own Children, and what more dear to you?
Thoſe that are the Support of your
own Families and the Church of
God too, and what greater Concern can there be? Your own
Welfare and theirs, the Proſperity
of your Families, and the Church's
too, depends very much upon your
Care. It is very much in your
Power

Power to make your selves and them, and all happy. The chief Concern indeed is put into better hands, those of the blessed Spirit ; but your Subserviency is required Fellow Workers together with him

You profess Love to the Lord Jesus, shew it by your espousing his Cause, and promoting his Interest, in preparing a Seed to serve him It is for your selves, it is for your dear Lord Jesus Let me beseech you, for the Love of Christ, to be observant and faithful

Herein you will be publickly useful, serviceable to the present and future Generations, as far as the Holy Seed shall be propagated It may be to Thousands and ten Thousands, these may arise and call you blessed

All good Men are concerned about a Protestant Succession in the Nation, and worthy it is of the Labours and Thoughts of all, and that not only for their own sakes, but for the sakes of their poor Children · Is not a Concern too about a religious Succession in your own Families highly becoming you, that

a

a Holy Family-Seed may be rais'd
fuitable to a National Proteftant
Succeffion? Evidence that your
Concern for the Publick is fincere,
by your Concern for thofe of your
own Houfe

What an Honour is put upon
you, to be the Inftruments of raifing and propagating a Seed to the
Lord Jefus? And what an Honour will it be in the Great Day of
the Lord, to ftand as a publick
Head to a glorious holy Progeny
By no means negle&t your Honour
and theirs

What if any fhould mifcarry
through your Negle&t? Is not the
thought of it terrible, that a Branch
in your Families fhould be cor-
rupted, and through you too?
And the Lofs of one may prove
the Lofs of Hundreds. Thus Ir-
religion may be propagated, and
Multitudes loft thro' your default
———Thefe either prove the beft or
worft of Men, the greateft Bleffings or the greateft Curfes. If not
an Eminent Seed for Chrift, they
ufually prove a Notorious Seed for
Satan; either Props and Pillars of
Reli-

Religious Families, or Undermi-
ners of them · For when left of
God, they commonly become the
moft violent Oppofers of Religion,
and the greateft Enemies to Chrift.
So much the greater Care ought to
be had of them.

And laftly, When was there an
Age in which the Seed was more
expofed ? The World lies in Wic-
kednefs How have Atheifm, Pro-
fanenefs, and Immorality o'er run
it ? There are Swarms every where
of Men of moft corrupt Principles
and Practices And how many
already are turned after Satan !
How many Religious Families are
either become Formalifts or De-
bauch'd ; yea, where's the profef-
fing Family that hath not an *Efau*
in it ? Is it not Time to concern
your felves ?

Wherefore let me intreat you as
Fathers, to take Care of the great
Charge that is put into your Hands,
as you will anfwer it to your Dear
Lord. Be early in a Religious Dedication of them to God, in the
moft folemn Manner devote them
to the Service of the Father, Son,
and

and Spirit. Bring your *Samuels* to God, and leave them with him. God hath put them into your Hands, they are one with you. You are clothed with Power and Authority from God to transact their Concerns in their Minority. What can you do lefs for their Souls, than in the moft ferious Manner to devote them to God. Let them be caft upon the Lord from the Womb. Don't dare to think, or fay, you will leave them to the Grace of God to work on them : You may as well fay, you will leave them to the Providence of God to maintain them, and fo expofe Soul and Body together. And how will you approve your felves finccre with God in your Co-venanting with him, if you leave out fo confiderable a Part of what is your own, your Children and all muft be devoted to God, *the only way to fave all, is to leave all with God.*

And then improve an early Dedication by repeated Cries and renewed Refignations of them to God. *As oft as you renew your Cove-nants,* ʀʌ*nts,* ʌ*emember the poor Seed.* As they are capable, let them have ſuitable and Religious Inſtructions. See that they are well principled, which will be a mighty Antidote againſt common Infections. Take particular heed of running them into Temptations, out of a vain Ambition of their Preferment. 'Tis a fearful Truth, the moſt that miſcarry, miſcarry thro' the Neglect of theſe Duties.

V. We may hence learn the **Duty of the Children of good Parents.** *Your Work is to keep up Religion in your Families, in your Generation, and to tranſmit it yet further to the Ages to come.* Ariſe and be doing, and the Lord be with you. I intreat you, I charge you, prepare your ſelves for Service, and be active in it. I would thus argue with you.

Whom will you ſerve, if not the Lord Jeſus? Is there a better Maſter? Can you make a better Choice, than what hath been made for you? Doth he not deſerve your beſt Services, that left his Throne, and pour'd out his Soul to Death for you, and hath call'd you

F   with

with an high and honourable Calling, hath Chosen you as a Seed to serve him? O leave not his Service for the Drudgery of this World, and the God of it: You will dearly repent it, if you do

Is not your Lot fallen happily, who are born in Religious Families? What a glorious Priviledge is it to be the Children of good Parents, the Children of many Prayers, the Children of Religious Education, and the best Instructions? You are born at the very Gates of Heaven, will you arise to cancel an early Dedication to God? Will you arise to cross the Prayers of your Parents, and contradict what they have done for you, in the most tender Love to your Souls? will you try to overturn the Promises, and oppose the Work of a Redeemer? Take heed what you do, as you are born among the Stars, your Fall will be the more dreadful.

Have not you been devoted to God? Can you, dare you go back? At your Peril be it. Can you without Sacrilege alienate your selves from the Service of God?

And

And is that a trifling Crime? How will you anſwer it to God, and your good Parents in the Great Day? Is there not great Dependance upon your Well-doing? The Hopes of Parents, the Expectations of Miniſters, nay of God and Chriſt, are from you   If you prove faulty, how many Expectations will be cut off? Don't dare to impoſe on God and Man.

The Proſperity of *Zion* in ſome meaſure depends upon your Holineſs and Zeal   A Breach is made in her Walls, a Gate thrown open to the Enemy upon the Revolt of the Poſterity of the Righteous   A conſiderable Poſt is delivered up, and what may be the Conſequence? One Revolt and Deficiency may occaſion more, and where may it end? and all will be chargeable upon you

You are the Terror of Enemies, as well as the Hope of Friends   Satan fears you moſt, he employs his Agents in the firſt place to corrupt you.

Hereby he ſtrikes at the very Foundation   Your Negligence and

F 2   Car-

Carnality will gratify the Enemy moft, and put an Opportunity in his hands of advancing his defperate and bloody Defigns againft the Intereft of Chrift and Souls in the World. And is it nothing to join in with Satan againft the Great God and your dear Redeemer? It will be found dreadful Work at laft.

Is not there need of your Service? Many are revolted, fome are cut off by Death 'Tis alas! *a Day of fmall things*. Is it not time for you to put to your helping Hand? The Enemy advanceth, Religion is under a vifible Eclipfe, and a fenfible Decay Come, come, arife and build, and have the Honour of being *Repairers of Breaches, and Reftorers of Paths to dwell in*.

I am forc'd to fpeak feelingly to fome of you. Death hath fetch'd one from among you There's one flain on the Right Hand, and on the left; One Beloved and Valued; one Serious and Hopeful A wide Breach is made; who arifeth to fill it up? You are left behind

O

Of all Loves I intreat you, with all Authority I command you to arife and work. The Funeral might have been your own What are you left behind for? You have your own Room, and another's to fill up O ftrive who fhall be firft in their Preparations, and greateft in their Service Fain would I raife this Ambition in you

Are you fure of many Years? Your time of Service may be but fhort Begin now; lofe not one Day; the fame Meffenger that hath fetch'd your Friend and Companion, may quickly be order'd for you Let me mind you of what the Philofopher faid to one that afk'd him what he was a doing? He anfwer'd, *Paulatim morior*, I am a dying continually You cannot think fure, becaufe of the Brisknefs of Youth, you are fafe from Death, when one among your fclves hath fo lately, in a few Days, been wrefted out of your Arms and Embraces You are dying, 'tis time to work.

F 3 Have.

Have not some of you felt the Powers of the World to come? I am perswaded you have been often under the awakening Convictions of the Spirit of God Do I press you to any thing that your own Consciences and the Spirit of God have not been engaging you to; have you not tasted that the Lord is gracious? Take heed of *beginning in the Spirit, and ending in the Flesh.* 'Tis better you had never known the Ways of God, than that you should wickedly depart from him.

And to conclude, If this will not move you; know that if you revolt, God will call in others; his Son shall have a Seed to serve him. When the Jews apostatiz'd, the Gentiles were call'd in; and when one professing Family fails, the Grace of God will raise another. Can you be content that others should arise and build upon your Ruin? Are you willing to resign up your Glory to Strangers? O! *Let not another take your Crown* I would hope better things of you, tho' I thus speak, even what accompanies Salvation.

And

And laſt of all, we may infer, that *The Loſs of the Holy Seed is a very ſore, and dreadful, and general Loſs;* eſpecially when capacitated, and growing ripe for Service. This is a very complicated Loſs: A Loſs as univerſal as the Service which was expeƈted.

Which brings me to take a ſorrowful View of our own great Loſs we lament this Day: A Family-Loſs: A School Loſs: The Church's Loſs: The Nation's Loſs: A Generation's Loſs: The Miniſtry's Loſs

Which will appear, if we conſider, that the Deceaſed, beſides his natural and acquir'd Capacities, which were none of the leaſt, was in ſome extraordinary manner qualified for that Service: If we regard,

1. *His Temper;* which was mild and calm; even and tender; kind and compaſſionate. Tho' he hath liv'd with me twice ſeven Years, I cannot recolleƈt that I ever ſaw him in a Paſſion. His Carriage was ſo obliging and inoffenſive, that all that knew him lov'd him.

A

A very rare Character He was fo prudent and cautious, and fo far from Art and Guile, that I may fay, Whom did he ever offend by an intermedling Humor? And as he liv'd, fo he died, in a perfect Calm. Now what a great Ornament is fo good a Temper to Religion? What a neceffary Qualification to the Miniftry? Of all Men, Minifters have moft need of fuch an one *How bright doth Grace fhine in a good Difpofition?* even like the Sun in a ferene Day: This is ftrangely eclips'd in an ill Temper, and really difappears, as the Sun wading under a dark Cloud. But what made his Temper the more glorious, was,

2 *His Grace* This was what he defir'd above all; he fo lov'd Chrift, that he endeavour'd what he could to perfwade others to love him too I have heard fome thanking God, that they ever knew him. He began betimes to preach Chrift in his private Converfation, who never liv'd to preach him in any publick Congregation His Life was fo free from Stains, and his

Defires

Defires after Grace fo fervent and practical, that I cannot but think he was fincerely Gracious betimes: Efpecially when I reflect upon,

3. That *Spirit of Prayer* he had. He was frequent, and enlarg'd in his Duty. I have fometimes heard him fo heavenly and rais'd, that I have been afhamed of my felf, that one of his Years fhould be fo lively, and I fo dull. It is but rare in one of his Age, before he undertakes a Journey, to fpend a whole Day in Fafting and Prayer, that he may be kept from the Temptations of the Places where he was going. It is but rare for one of his Age, when in a Journey, to rife in the Night, (as *David* of old) to redeem Time for Prayer, which I am fatisfied he hath done. How was he us'd to be rapt up in another World in Prayer! I am fure our Family hath loft more ferious Prayers every Week, than there are Mornings and Evenings in it. I am fure I have loft the Advantage of many fervent Cries, he offer'd particularly upon my Account; which I have Reafon, to value the more, because of

4. *His*

4. *His choice Experiences.* These he hath left as a Legacy, under his own Hand; and 'tis a very choice one to me, worthy, I think, of every ones Attendance, but too large to be recounted now, I shall therefore only say; that tho' young, he was acquainted with the Comforts and Joys of the Holy Ghost; which many twice his Age, are utterly Strangers to He was in his Element when he was speaking about another World. It is said of *Alexander,* that *he recokn'd his Age by his Victories* If we may reckon the Age of our deceased Friend by his Duties, and Prayers, and Acquaintance with another World, we may say of him, *He liv'd long in a little Time.* He was preparing carefully to attend at the Lord's Table, which only a humble Sense of his own Unworthiness had hindred him from He prepar'd for the lower Table, but I trust he is gone to the upper Table, to receive there: He was laying in a Stock to serve his Lord on Earth, but is (I hope) remov'd to serve about the Throne, where Thousands of Thousands,

ſands, and **Ten Thouſands of Ten Thouſands,** are adoring him that ſits upon the **Throne, and the Lamb,** for ever and ever. *Amen.*

F I N I S.

BOOKS printed for *N Cliff*, at the *Bible* and *Three Crowns*, in *Cheapſide*, near *Mercers-Chappel.*

1 COmmentaries on the Holy Bible. 2. A Method for Prayer, with Scripture-Expreſſions proper to be uſed under each Head. 3. Some Forms of Prayer for the Uſe of Families and private Perſons, taken out of Mr *Henry*'s Method for Prayer. To which are added by the ſame Author, Prayers before and after Receiving the Lord's Supper. Price 3 Pence, or 20 Shillings a Hundred. 4. Diſputes Reviewed In a mon preached at the Evening Lecture at *Salters-Hall,* on the Lord's Day, *July* 23. 1710. 5 A Sermon concerning the Succeſs of the Miniſtry Preach'd at the *Tueſday* Lecture at *Salters-Hall,* *July,* 25. 1710. 6 The Communicant's Companion Or, Inſtructions and Helps for the right Receiving of the Lord's Supper The Fourth Edition corrected. 7 *Great Britain*'s preſent Joys and Hopes · Open'd in two Sermons, preach'd in *Cheſter*; the former on the National Thankſgiving-
Day,

Day, *December* 31. 1706. The latter the Day following being *New-Years-Day.* 8. A Sermon concerning the right Management of friendly Visits. 9. A Church in the House · A Sermon concerning Family - Religion. 10. A Discourse concerning Meekness and Quietness of Spirit, to which is added, A Sermon on *Acts* 28. 22. Shewing that the Christian Religion is not a Sect, and yet that it is every where spoken against. 11. A Scripture Catechism, in the Method of the Assemblies. 12. Two Funeral Sermons, one on Dr. *Samuel Benion,* and the other on the Reverend Mr. *Francis Talents,* Ministers of the Gospel in *Shrewsbury,* with a short Account of their Lives. 13 A Sermon concerning the Forgiveness of Sin as a Debt. Publish'd with some Enlargements at the Request of some who heard it. Preach'd in *London, June* 1. 1711. *All Written by Mr.* Matthew Henry, *Minister of the Gospel.*

An Account of some remarkable Passages in the Life of a private Gentleman, with Reflections thereon, in three Parts, relating to Trouble of Mind, some violent Temptations, and a Recovery, in order to awaken the Presumptuous, convince the Sceptick, and encourage the Despondent Left under his own Hand, to be communicated to the publick, after his Decease. The Second Edition with Additions from the Author's original Papers.

Lightning Source UK Ltd.
Milton Keynes UK
UKHW022035160720
366673UK00013B/268